MIXED SIGNALS

Richard Parker

MIXED SIGNALS

THE PROSPECTS FOR GLOBAL TELEVISION NEWS

A TWENTIETH CENTURY FUND REPORT

THE TWENTIETH CENTURY FUND PRESS ◆ NEW YORK ◆ 1995

Published in association with the Joan Shorenstein Center on the Press, Politics and Public Policy, John F. Kennedy School of Government, Harvard University.

Library of Congress Cataloging-in-Publication Data

Parker, Richard,   1946–
    Mixed signals : the prospects for global television news / by
    Richard Parker.
        p.   cm.
    Includes index.
    ISBN 0-87078-374-2   (alk. paper)
    1.   Television broadcasting of news--Social aspects.
    2.   Journalistic ethics.   I. Title.
PN4784.T4P37   1995
070.1'95--dc20

                                                                95–19651
                                                                CIP

Cover design and illustration: Claude Goodwin
Manufactured in the United States of America.
Copyright © 1995 by the Twentieth Century Fund, Inc.

Foreword

Among the paradoxes of the modern world, none is more jarring than the combination of the continuing growth of an international economy and culture on the one hand, and the persistence of the most narrow and even pernicious divisions among human beings on the other. In Sarajevo, for example, multinational news organizations can festoon the city with satellite uplinks, but the war they are reporting on reminds us how close we still are to our tribal origins. From a long-run perspective, of course, the forces of modernization and technological change seem immensely powerful and even inevitable. Policymakers and scholars observing the current phase of the parade to the future must find ways to comprehend the scale and calculate the pace of change—while preserving a healthy regard for human stubbornness and habits of mind.

This balance is particularly valuable in understanding the prospects for global television news. The explosion of television viewership in the last several decades is undeniable, albeit important differences persist based on national wealth. And, the spread of remarkable new technologies, especially cable systems and satellite dishes, means that the next generation of the medium will take a new form. Moreover, the opening of whole societies to commercial and foreign broadcasting seems another potent force for change.

The Twentieth Century Fund, in recent years, has taken the view that the media constitute a natural field of study for an institution focused on politics and public policy. As a result, we have sponsored several studies intended to help government officials and the interested public understand the implications of some of these new developments. In 1991, we published Anthony Smith's *The Age of Behemoths*, a study of the concentration of media ownership. Today, controversies over concentration of ownership abound. As this report goes to press, for example, both Britain and Italy are moving to limit the degree of concentration in their media. Meanwhile, the United States, characteristically in the current era of dominance by pure

v

market philosophy, is moving to expand the range of permitted activities by individual companies. Recently, the Federal Communications Commission in effect acquiesced in a de facto violation of foreign ownership rules for television in the Rupert Murdoch case.

In 1992, Lewis A. Friedland's Fund paper, *Covering the World*, explored the international television news services. Friedland pointed out that different news organizations throughout the world relied on the same sources for their videotaped images, suggesting the potential for common experience. Friedland made clear, however, that even if the picture itself is often the story, the different languages and perspectives of the reporters and their audiences make somewhat different interpretations more the rule than the exception.

In a sense, this report by Richard Parker, senior fellow and lecturer at Harvard University's Kennedy School of Government, continues and broadens the discussion presented by Friedland. Parker suggests that, quite apart from differences in news judgment or local perspective, language is likely to be the decisively limiting factor in the globalization of news for the foreseeable future. He in no sense seeks to diminish the significance of live pictures transmitted of Tiananmen Square or of missiles in flight during the Gulf War. Rather, he argues that common sources of tape footage are a far cry from a universal news outlet.

Parker also puts in perspective the reach and viewership of existing international news services such as CNN International, the BBC World Service, and Sky Channel. It is worth noting that the BBC radio version has been available in forty-one languages for many years, providing extremely high-quality news and arts programming to an estimated worldwide audience of 130 million.

In an era of diminished global ideological competition, tight governmental budgets, and increasingly privatized television, Parker emphasizes that the same economic considerations that shape entertainment television will drive the development of news broadcasting. In the United States, surely the "leader" in commercialized television, the shift in news content and emphasis in recent years is obvious. The process aptly termed the "tabloidization" of news coverage is well advanced. It may be too strong to say that this development merely reflects that what gets on the air is what sells, but only by a little. In this sense, there will be globalized news when it can turn a profit by becoming a more effective commercial vehicle for selling things.

Parker does not deny the significance of the new technologies, particularly satellite television. He points out, however, that along with the possibilities for commercial exploitation through news or entertainment programming, technology also must be assessed soberly in the light of national tastes, language, laws, income, and so forth.

Parker argues persuasively that "the relativity of language and culture is acting as a powerful gatekeeper." He also makes clear that the basic economics of television (both in terms of viewer income and marketing techniques) works to dampen the surge of international news production and dissemination. The great advances in the latter—we take for granted today the ability to beam news anywhere on the globe—may have sent false signals about the potential audience for this sort of programming. There is still no real evidence of a mass audience for news in another language with a foreign spin.

Parker invites us to consider another possibility: the new technologies will provide viewers with potentially hundreds of channels and thus the ability to choose very narrowly among many potential programs. In these circumstances, it is possible that a substantial fraction of the audience may choose news with an even more exclusively local flavor and idiom than it has today.

This work was cosponsored by the Joan Shorenstein Center on the Press, Politics and Public Policy at the John F. Kennedy School of Government, Harvard University. On behalf of the Center and the Trustees of the Twentieth Century Fund, I thank Richard Parker for his contribution to this important area.

RICHARD C. LEONE, *President*
The Twentieth Century Fund
July 1995

Contents

ACKNOWLEDGMENTS

The author wishes to acknowledge the following individuals for their help and insights, while at the same time relieving them of responsibility for errors and omissions which are the author's own: Peter Vesey, vice president, Cable Network News International; Jean-Luc Renaud, Logica Consulting; Rich Zahradnik, editor, Television Business International; George Dessart, International Academy of Television Arts and Sciences; Professor Hal Himmelstein, Center for World Television, Brooklyn College; Scott Goodfellow, Goodfellow & Co.; Les Brown, Center for Communication Studies; Neil Weinstock, Frost & Sullivan; William Kovach, Director, Neiman Foundation, Harvard University; Dr. Oswald Ganley, Executive Director, Program on Information Resources Policy, Harvard University; Chris Irwin, president, and Hugh Williams, vice president, BBC World Service Television; Robert Kennedy, deputy director, Middle East Broadcasting Center; Leonard Sussman, Freedom House; John Pavlik, associate director, Freedom Forum, Columbia University; Arthur Green, Wildovsky & Green; Enrique Jara, president, Reuters TV; Professor Russell Neuman, Tufts University; David Bartlett, executive director, Association of Radio-TV News Directors; Ken Koyne, chairman, WTN.

I additionally want to thank Marvin Kalb, director of the Joan Shorenstein Center on the Press, Politics, and Public Policy, and Ellen Hume, the Center's former executive director, for their unfailing support for my research and teaching, as well as Richard C. Leone, president, and the staff of the Twentieth Century Fund, for their financial support.

Most importantly, I must thank my wife, Robin Wright, and son, Samuel, for their unstinting patience and understanding—my debt to them is unredeemable.

Introduction

Ted Turner's satellite television news service, CNN International, was launched less than a decade ago. Today, its signal can be received in more than 200 countries, comprising more than five billion of the earth's inhabitants. The BBC's World Service Television, a recent challenge to Turner's Atlanta-based network, already broadcasts to four continents. Rupert Murdoch has just added Hong Kong-based Star TV—whose satellite footprint stretches from the Mediterranean to the Western Pacific—to a television empire that already includes the Fox television network in the United States and BSkyB in Europe. In Latin America, CNN, NBC, and Mexican giant Televisa are all competing over audiences for their satellite-based news coverage. In Africa, South Africa's M-Net now blankets the continent. Throughout the Arab World, the London-based Middle East Broadcast Center now beams down its signal twenty-four hours a day.

Satellite-based television news services today can be seen on every continent. The establishment of this new industry—in less than a decade—has startled media critics. It has also set off a flurry of activity among giant media companies, with talk of integration and "global synergy" as the next step in the evolution of television. The idea that—in theory, at least—the same news (or entertainment or sports) program can be watched simultaneously in Kansas, Kazakhstan, and the Kalahari is certainly startling.

But how will this programming, which is technologically feasible today, actually enter the daily reality of the earth's inhabitants? The twentieth century is full of technological breakthroughs that have yet to reach much of the world's populace—from telephones to air conditioners, jet planes to laser surgery. The West easily forgets that 60 percent of the earth's inhabitants have never even made a phone call, and that more than half have no ongoing access to electricity.

This paper looks at some of the gatekeeping issues that will shape the evolution of global television—and especially television news. Globally, the great majority of people still don't watch television regularly; and in most countries, when they do watch, they see programming delivered by a government monopoly. Although the past decade has brought major growth in private channels (especially in Europe and Latin America), no public broadcaster has yet gone out of business. And because television is such a powerful and culturally sensitive medium, as well as the source of great wealth to those who control it, governments nowhere show signs of divesting the power to regulate and modify what is shown inside their borders.

In principle, by beaming its signal down to individual home dish receivers, satellite-based television can bypass national governments and their restrictions, opening a cornucopia of program alternatives to viewers. Yet to date, the upsurge in viewership for international broadcasting—via satellite and cable—is, with few exceptions, at much lower levels than popularly imagined. Although satellites may make such broadcasts theoretically available on all continents, the number of homes equipped to receive such signals isn't yet half of 1 percent.

Moreover, in countries with competitive broadcasting, viewers, to a greater extent than once imagined, prefer to watch television produced and presented in their native language by people who look and act like them and reflect values similar to their own. This discovery—implying ongoing importance for discreet national (or linguistic) markets—has influenced advertiser interest in global television, as the elusiveness of global consumer markets has become more apparent. It also reveals the forces shaping the broadcasters' alternative revenue streams—viewer subscriptions and cable fees—as viewers increasingly choose television in their vernacular. At the same time, perceiving a challenge from international competitors, national broadcast systems—public and private—are using the same satellite and cable technology to secure the loyalty of their native audiences. In Asia alone, nearly a dozen single-country satellites are scheduled for launch in the next two years.

From all this, one can't conclude that global television will fail as an enterprise, but one can conclude that the path ahead won't be as simple or straightforward as the technology's potential recently suggested. This study attempts to examine—and evaluate—some of the signposts along that path.

1

THE PROMISE—AND CHALLENGE—OF GLOBAL TELEVISION

Television, over the past four decades, has transformed the ways we think about, talk about, or even imagine, the news. A century ago, news—in the modern sense—was still primarily the privilege of the literate, who garnered it from newspapers. The papers in turn had only recently (and unevenly) started to use the telegraph to carry news of distant events quickly to editors' desks. Where the telegraph did not yet reach—an expanse covering much of the planet in the late nineteenth century—the "news" still traveled by post, or ship, or even horseback, and far from being new, might be days or weeks old by the time it reached a newspaper's front page.

The advent of radio in the 1920s and 1930s—with its ability to broadcast events (in some cases, "live"), to span vast distances instantaneously, and most important, to be accessible to those who couldn't read—marked a quantum leap in news coverage and dissemination. But radio's primacy, in the industrial countries at least, was short-lived. Soon after World War II ended, television burst forth, reshaping the news roles of both newspapers and radio.

Television news shared immediacy with radio, but uniquely offered us the ability to "see" events unfold ten blocks—or ten thousand miles—away. The world, it sometimes seemed, had come into our living rooms. But in a century saturated with technological novelty, television's innovation, like so many others, has grown commonplace.

Today, however, we seem poised for another momentous shift. This new quantum leap goes by several names; most commonly, it's referred to as "global" or "borderless" television, and a great many newscasters, media moguls, and media critics alike insist that this global aspect represents an unprecedented future for television—especially

3

television news. Officials at CNN—the best known example of this new globalism—like to describe their network as "the creator of Marshall McLuhan's electronic global village" and "the world's only twenty-four-hour global television network."[1] But what precisely *is* global television?

Most dramatically, global television includes the live broadcast of students lying down before tanks in Tiananmen Square, or of troops faced with unarmed civilians outside the Russian White House, or from the warhead cameras of cruise missiles in flight during the Gulf War.

All of these distant events were affected by being broadcast live— not only were we drawn directly into the struggles they represented, but because we were watching, the coverage became a factor in the events themselves as leaders and participants alike used television to shape demands, appeal for support, and gauge the strength and commitment of their opponents. There was a less visible, if no less powerful, effect as well; "we" as an audience were in some sense changed, too—aware (as were the event's participants) that what we saw was being seen simultaneously in more than a hundred countries around the world.

This dramatic element of global television coverage—the extraordinary ability of lightweight, hand-held cameras linked to suitcase-sized ground transmitters to broadcast events not just live, but into hundreds of millions of homes around the world—has become a part of modern events, an essential component in the very grammar of change. Indeed, this instantaneous globalism is now so imminent in the discussion of coverage of world events that many newspeople are now wondering what responsibilities new global television journalists and television news organizations have toward their massive, cross-cultural audiences.[2]

The idea of global television, though, concerns more than just news coverage of singular moments or events delivered to a mass, universal audience. First of all, it is based on a much-discussed technological revolution—the dawn, its proponents argue, of an Electronic Age that is swiftly displacing the Industrial Era. As part of this new age, television is being reborn in a world of satellites and home satellite dishes, of copper and fiber-optics cable, of (soon, we are told) a nearly unlimited number of channels, and of high-definition reception and virtual reality and digitization and interactivity. And through that technological transformation, the new globalism will, the experts promise, finally offer us a global programming menu of game shows, shopping channels, sports, movies, sitcoms, "soft" news, and even "soft" porn— a cornucopia of information and entertainment, education and sweetly simple diversions.

But most important, at its core, global television implies something quite profound. If it succeeds, it represents the foundations of a common universal culture, in which we will someday see much the same programming no matter where we live—a final, dialectic completion of the century-old notion of mass culture. Economically, it implies an equally expansive vision, a capitalist *sanctum sanctorum* in effect—the ultimate mass market not only for global programming, but for global advertising, global products, and global consumer spending as well. Linked together through these common, invented "vernaculars," proponents tell us we stand literally on the edge of an era when (no matter where we live) we will be able, at the flick of a button, to satisfy whatever interest, appetite, or fantasy we might have. But *is* this in fact where we're heading? Are we all about to enter a century in which satellites humming above us will bounce back identical and instantaneous information and entertainment whether we're in Kalamazoo or the Kalahari?

The *promise* of such a future appears unmistakable, at least to many. CNN International can already be seen in more than 200 countries; more than 120 communication satellites now beam television pictures down to every inhabited continent; the number of television sets in use has more than doubled since 1985, and now exceeds 1.2 billion globally; and that symbolic cornerstone of the internationalized, yet individualized, television future—the simple parabolic "home dish" receiver—may soon be almost as small and inexpensive as a television today.

Oxford political scientist Timothy Garton-Ash, watching television's impact on Eastern Europe as the Soviet empire crumbled, in awe pronounced television "the world's third superpower." Today, a host of anecdotal evidence points toward much the same conclusion, if in sometimes disarming ways. Consider:

▲ In Japanese homes today, televisions are more common than flush toilets.

▲ During the Gulf War, Iraqi troops carted off an estimated 50,000 satellite dishes—leading some CNN staffers to joke that what the Iraqis wanted wasn't oil, but free television.

▲ In New Delhi, Shanghai, and other large Asian cities, thousands of local entrepreneurs have nailed satellite receivers to crowded apartment buildings, making pirated satellite channels—from MTV to Dynasty—available to millions of local residents.

▲   Filipino troops recently were able to surprise and capture a gueril-
    la mountain camp because its revolutionary inhabitants were too
    busy watching MTV.

▲   *Los Simpsons* is now a top-rated show in Colombia and Argentina,
    while a Mexican soap opera, *The Rich Also Cry*, is winning massive
    audiences in Moscow.

▲   The United States alone now exports more than 120,000 hours of
    television program annually just to Europe—double the amount
    only six years ago. In toto, global trade in programming is grow-
    ing at more than 15 percent per year.[3]

Little wonder then that John Eger, a former CBS executive and
White House telecommunications policy chief, could rhapsodize
recently on his industry's future:

> [Global television is] a technology that knows no barriers,
> no national boundaries and does not recognize any of the
> artificial divisions between the different people and places
> of the world. Here is a technology that does not recognize
> color, creed, race, or nationality. It is a technology that is
> supernational, acultural, alingual, a technology of sight
> and sound, of binary digits, that can indeed saturate the
> world.
>   It is a technology that creates simply by providing the
> means—a flow of information and ideas—a force throughout
> the world that simply will not stop, however we may resist
> its flow. . . . [Global television] is a truly vast and revolution-
> ary change, propelled by our technology towards acceptance
> of the concept that we are indeed one people on Earth, one
> family living in one home, a family with common problems,
> concerns, and interests.[4]

By contrast, Silvio Berlusconi, formerly president of the international media conglomerate Fininvest Group (and briefly Italy's prime
minister), sees the future for global television as decidedly more complicated and tentative than Eger would allow. Berlusconi claims to agree
roughly with the broadly popular notion that the future belongs to global television. But he then quickly insists that its arrival lies off in a distant, and uncertain, future. "That future will be a long time coming," he
says. "Not years but maybe decades, maybe more than a century." And

in a direct warning to the Egers of the world, Berlusconi insists (in answer to his own questions about the new globalism):

> Doesn't Ted Turner's CNN broadcast news for the world at large? Don't Rupert Murdoch's satellite ventures represent a major step toward the Global Village? *The answer is no.*[5]

Berlusconi's perception about both time horizons and about the implications of current innovations such as Turner's CNN and Murdoch's Sky News and Star TV are echoed in Peter Fiddick's assessment of the same unfolding process. Fiddick is editor of the distinguished British media journal, the *Listener*, and to him much about the cheerful predictions of borderless television conceals a quite nationalistic and corporatist struggle over control of potentially vast new wealth:

> Forget the Global Village. . . . [W]e are demonstrating, in a megabuck frenzy of media activity that spans at least two continents, that despite it all we are little more than a random encounter of parochial nation states.[6]

To Fiddick, all too much of the talk about globalization is a corporate form of happy talk, as international media giants go about the process of reorganizing and capturing control of new media markets and assets. Far from inaugurating an era that knows no "color, creed, race, or nationality," something decidedly more mundane—and suspiciously venal—is at work in this global expansion of media giants:

> In some cases we see the preemptive strike in action, as some media group stakes out a piece of territory to ensure against having to pay twice the price to retrieve it from a rival at some unknown future date. . . . Others, more versed in the niceties of mediaspeak, talk of the need to form an integrated network—vertically, horizontally, you name it—capable of giving a flexible response to the demands of the 21st century and so forth, when what they are really doing is more to do with getting big enough to be bid-proof.[7]

Berlusconi is preeminently a businessman, Fiddick a media critic, but what both are pointing out is that, ultimately, global television—whatever its technological origins—is going to be profoundly affected by the emerging market economics and the market actors that increasingly shape television around the world.

The coverage of the Gulf War—considered the new medium's crowning moment to date—offers one precise set of lessons about why technology alone won't determine global television's future. Although war coverage, including Peter Arnett's on-the-scene coverage from Baghdad, earned both plaudits and a vastly expanded audience for CNN during the height of the war, Ted Turner's network quickly discovered two discomfiting things.

First, the audience for this particular form of global television news proved transient. Shortly after the war's end, CNN's viewership promptly returned to prewar levels, only a fraction of that of the big U.S. networks. Second, the coverage itself proved crushingly expensive—news executives in fact were horrified. "No network is in a position to spend two, three and four million dollars a month to remain on a war footing," Eason Jordan, managing editor of CNN's international desk, admitted. At CBS, one vice president went further: the much richer network's Gulf operations took a proportionately higher percentage of the CBS News budget "than any other story we've covered in my memory."[8] Along with ABC and NBC, CBS continues to cut back on overseas bureaus, at the very moment proponents see the global market as exploding.

Television around the globe is going through a host of changes simultaneously. The most popularly understood, of course, are driven by the wonders of satellites and cable, fiber optics, high-definition television (HDTV), interactivity, and the like—the technology that captures the imagination. But what the microcosm of the Gulf War coverage made clear are the political-economic decisions that governments and private corporations will have to make if the technology is ever to become a meaningful reality.

To Americans, acknowledging the role of markets and competition in television might seem commonplace. But it's crucial to understand the novelty of market economics shaping global television's development. For much of television's first forty years (outside the United States),[9] the world of television was fundamentally one of government-owned stations broadcasting on as few as one or two channels. From the 1950s up to the mid-1980s, economics—in the sense of competitive market economics—played little or no role, since the governments operated their television systems as public agencies. Sustained by a combination of taxes and viewer fees, advertising and competition between channels played virtually no part in television's global development.

But in the future, what role is economics going to play? How will it shape the emergence of global television, and in particular, development of television news—the medium the majority in industrialized countries now consider their primary news source? Will competition and privatization of television open up new and competing sources of information? Will direct access by satellite act to erode authoritarian regimes, playing a role similar to that of shortwave during World War II and the cold war? Will a handful of corporate owners emerge to dominate the new world? Will the flow of information become so truly diversified that the indictments once embodied in the New World Information Order come to have no meaning? Will the average citizen in rural Africa or Asia find herself as able to be "informed" about the events and issues of the day as a government official or stockbroker in Washington, Tokyo, or London?

None of these questions offers simple answers. Indeed, despite the overwhelming importance of such issues, most researchers would agree that the entire field is hobbled by fragmentary data, rapidly changing conditions, and simple confusion about current trends and their future implications. As one American network executive told me in the course of research, "The problem with most academic studies is they're usually out of date by the time they're published, and the business research either asks the wrong questions—if you want a global overview—or relies on data we sometimes don't trust ourselves." Within those obvious limitations, this paper attempts to address the following questions:

▲   What forces are acting on technology to shape its application in the global television market?

▲   Is the 1980s' belief that private actors will swiftly overcome the tradition of government control of television in most countries as likely as it once seemed?

▲   Given the undeniable growth of privately owned television systems—terrestrial, satellite, and cable—what impact is that growth having on programming choice, industry organization, and public-private competition?

▲   What impact is the increased choice that greater channel selection offers having on viewing patterns, particularly as it affects the international trade in entertainment programming and news flows?

▲   How are new patterns of program transmission—options such as cable and regional or global satellite—shaping, and being shaped by, advertising and viewer fees, in lieu of traditional public television taxes? Particularly in the area of news, are the new global and regional news networks—CNN International, BBC/WST, Sky News, Star TV, Euronews, MBC, and Televisa's ECO—displacing domestic news sources?

Answers to these questions are crucial to understanding and shaping the future market for global television, and judging whether we stand on the verge of a mass-audience, McLuhanesque global village—sharing in a common pool of programming—or something else.

2

Economics, Markets, Technology, and Television

Television is hardly the first vaunted "revolution" that industrialization has brought us. The electric light, telephone, radio, airplane, automobile, and phonograph are all examples of earlier technological innovations that form the cornerstones of the modern consumer society. Yet despite the global availability of these technologies (in some cases, for more than a century), Americans forget that well over half the planet's population enjoys no routine access to virtually any of them. As noted earlier, 60 percent of the world's inhabitants, for example, have never even made a phone call, and well over half have no electricity.[1]

Mass production of automobiles began in the United States and Western Europe before World War I. By the mid-1920s, cars were in use around the world—but at widely different levels. Today, seventy years later, the automobile is most certainly global—yet it is still used with much the same relative ranking of distribution as in the mid-1920s. In 1990, in the United States, the number of inhabitants per automobile was 1.8, and in Western Europe 2.6; but for Latin America, the figure was 45.9; in Africa, 358; and in Asia, 793.[2]

This distribution pattern highlights the difference between what economics refers to as "extensive" versus "intensive" factors. The automobile is today extensively present throughout the world, but intensively present in only a minority of affluent countries. Put another way, to talk of, say, Mercedes as having a global market is coherent in the sense that certainly Mercedes are driven in virtually every country on the planet; whether such a claim is meaningful—given the numbers driven, and by whom—is more open to doubt.

Whether it's washing machines or sewing machines, stereos or dishwashers, the West's common experience of easily accessible consumer

11

products (with an implied belief in the rough "egalitarianism" of such access) is still consistently belied by global data on household appliance and consumer electronics consumption.[3]

If technology is such a driving force in shaping the world of today, why should certain parts of the globe remain untouched? The simplest answer, in economic terms, is that the dispersion of new technologies follows markets—or the lack thereof. In the case of television's development, two crucial elements in market development have shaped dispersion to date: *distribution of income* and *government policy.*

INCOME DISTRIBUTION'S ROLE

For most people in most countries, individual or household income is the first crucial determinant of access to television (or autos, stereos, or other consumer goods). Indeed, most studies of television ownership country-by-country show how simply such ownership correlates with per capita income. High income means a high number of televisions per capita; low income means a low number.[4]

In the case of automobiles, there seems to be a takeoff point for demand in terms of income: studies find that, at about $2,000 per capita, countries become viable in terms of supporting a consumer automobile culture, although one significantly below American levels. For smaller consumer items, of course, the takeoff point in terms of cost-to-demand ratios is sharply lower. Black-and-white television sets, for example, can be manufactured below $100.

But here one encounters a second problem. Countries with low per capita incomes tend to be rural and have weak infrastructure. For such countries, the cost of large-scale electricity generation and distribution is high, hence making the cost to consumers of household electricity also high—when available. Yet it is in such countries where a majority of the world's population dwells, and where an estimated 85 percent of population growth will occur over the next thirty years.

Table 2.1 (see pages 14–15) gives a global overview of television sets and (for comparison) automobile usage per capita that lets us see this crucial first point about television quite clearly.

THE EFFECT OF GOVERNMENTS

While income plays a leading role in the distribution of basic access to television, government policy toward television has been the other chief determinant of television's evolution. Apart from the United States (and two or three other exceptions such as Monaco), virtually every country developed its television broadcast system as a government monopoly. Sometimes the system was a direct, ministerial part of the government, sometimes a semi-independent public agency (such as the BBC).[5]

In the excited talk about globalization and competition, it's sometimes forgotten how large these public systems still loom. Globally, the majority of people still live in countries where public broadcast monopolies have no domestic private competitors. In Western Europe and Latin America, and to a lesser extent, East Asia, although governments began allowing privately owned channels as competitors in the late 1970s and 1980s, these public systems today still play a major role in broadcast. In countries with "dual" public-private systems—such as Britain, Germany, Italy, or Japan—the public broadcaster still is more watched than any private competitor. In revenue terms, moreover, the largest public systems (such as the BBC, Italy's RAI, or Japan's NHK) rank with private media giants such as Cap Cities/ABC, NBC, or CBS, even though the U.S. market is substantially larger.[6]

To date, in more than 190 countries that began with public broadcast monopolies, none of those broadcasters has gone out of business.[7] In the fifty or so countries (primarily in Western Europe and Latin America) that now have dual public-private systems, there was a great deal of heated talk in the 1980s about public broadcasting becoming a dinosaur. Today, those same public systems show no signs of withering away. Quite to the contrary, charged with becoming more competitive, these public systems now accept advertising, use audience research, schedule programming, and generally behave as if they were private broadcasters.

As a consequence, although European public broadcasters in the 1980s experienced a sharp drop in audience share as new private channels proliferated, more recent studies show public stations holding their own. With only a handful of exceptions, in fact, the public channels still capture the majority of the viewing audience, even in the face of aggressive private competition.[8]

This survival—and in many countries, continued dominance—of the public broadcasters will greatly influence the evolution of global television patterns. Fundamentally committed to their national audiences, with a more complex mandate and agenda, and now increasingly competitive with private national alternatives, public broadcasters are shaping the markets—and market-entry terms—in a number of crucial ways for transnational broadcasting.

Eli Noam, in his comprehensive book *Television in Europe*, underscores this point in a way that applies outside Europe as well. Talking about the impact of private competitors, satellite and cable technology,

TABLE 2.1
KEY GLOBAL CONSUMER GOODS
(Number of People per Car, TV, Telephone, Radio)

REGION/COUNTRY	CAR	TV	TELEPHONE	RADIO
OECD	2.6	2.0	2.5	2.1
Australia	23.0	2.1	1.8	0.8
Canada	2.2	1.8	1.3	1.1
France	2.5	2.7	1.6	27.0
Greece	7.0	3.0	2.5	3.1
Italy	2.5	3.4	1.5	3.5
Japan	4.2	1.7	1.8	1.2
Spain	3.8	2.8	4.1	2.9
Sweden	2.5	35.0	1.0	2.5
Switzerland	2.4	2.8	1.2	2.5
United Kingdom	2.8	2.8	1.9	3.0
United States	1.8	1.2	1.3	0.5
EAST EUROPE	21.7	7.8	9.4	4.4
Hungary	6.4	13.0	16.2	6.8
Poland	9.0	4.4	8.5	3.9
Romania	81.1	4.0	—	6.9
Former Soviet Union	22.8	9.4	10.3	4.4
ASIA PACIFIC	139.5	20.4	24.4	6.5
Hong Kong	29.8	4.2	2.2	1.6
South Korea	50.7	5.2	5.4	1.0
Philippines	179.0	28.0	—	7.5
Singapore	10.7	4.7	2.3	3.3
Thailand	107.7	10.1	52.6	5.6
ASIAN PLANNED	1,106.4	135.5	185.7	7.5
China	1,093.3	100.7	149.8	7.1
Vietnam	29.8	531.3	9.8	—
SOUTH ASIA	794.9	172.0	258.5	142.0
India	542.4	155.0	191.0	12.9

REGION/COUNTRY	CAR	TV	TELEPHONE	RADIO
SUB-SAHARAN AFRICA	357.0	695.7	345.1	10.3
Ethiopia	1,122.4	607.2	339.9	5.4
Kenya	182.4	184.3	72.7	11.8
Mozambique	177.9	144.0	233.0	28.0
Nigeria	144.8	179.1	366.7	6.1
South Africa	11.4	9.1	6.9	2.2
Sudan	706.3	19.5	280.1	4.0
Zaire	354.2	2,100.0	765.5	10.5
Zimbabwe	56.2	64.7	32.8	17.5
MIDDLE EAST/ NORTH AFRICA	73.6	23.3	32.6	6.5
Egypt	125.5	12.4	35.6	33.0
Iran	33.3	19.2	26.5	4.5
Iraq	70.1	16.5	18.6	5.0
Israel	6.2	3.8	2.6	2.1
Kuwait	3.4	39.0	5.8	3.6
Morocco	44.2	19.4	69.2	4.9
Saudi Arabia	11.6	3.4	8.0	2.9
Syria	124.4	17.1	16.8	4.3
LATIN AMERICA/ CARIBBEAN	45.9	15.7	16.5	4.1
Argentina	7.8	4.6	9.7	1.5
Brazil	15.8	5.2	11.3	2.7
Chile	21.4	6.1	15.5	3.0
Cuba	533.5	5.0	18.9	3.0
Mexico	15.5	8.4	10.4	4.9
Nicaragua	109.9	17.0	63.4	3.9
Peru	54.5	43.3	41.1	6.1
Venezuela	11.7	7.2	11.3	2.3

Source: Adapted from *The Economist Vital World Statistics* (New York: Times Books, 1990), pp. 234–35.

and VCRs on Europe's public television in the 1980s, he cautions against viewing their effects simply as a product of technological innovation and private entrepreneurship:

> [T]he introduction of new forms of video distribution destabilized a system whose monopoly status was already under pressure. . . . [A]t the same time, it would be simplistic to view the availability of technology as a deus ex machina.
>
> Satellites would have become much less of a factor had not several major European countries adopted a political agenda of technology development. . . . Once [state-sponsored rockets and satellites] were technically operational they had to be put to good use to justify the effort.
>
> Similarly, in several countries cable television was actively pushed by the PTT [post, telephone, and telegraph] telecommunications monopolies as part of their expansion into new functions once they had successfully completed the spread of basic telephone service. . . . Entry into cable provided some protection from potential rivals in the future . . . and it served their affiliated equipment suppliers well. . . . Such efforts led to a proliferation of video channels, not as part of media or cultural policy, but as a result of economic and development policy in the electronics sector.

Noam goes on to emphasize that—contrary to the highly touted 1980s' vision of a technologically driven, privatized, and freely competitive global television system dominating the twenty-first century— the role of the public sector will loom large for a very long time:

> Broadcast media are part of our cultural reference and they help to set the political agenda-setting role. Competing groups vie for control over culture because it permits them to influence society. Thus, broadcasting institutions are often embroiled in controversy over values and politics. . . .
>
> In the process, however, neither governments nor public broadcasters will become obsolete. The latter continue to have important functions, in particular producing or distributing programs that are not adequately provided otherwise. They are experienced organizations with an important mission and wide support, and they will not vanish. They may even improve as the privileges of their exclusivity vanish.[9]

Government's direct hand in broadcasting is far from the only means by which it is shaping television. As Noam mentioned, governments have a myriad of means to affect profoundly the evolution of television well into the next century, at a minimum.

Through their PTT systems, for example, they can directly control (or set standards for) entry and operation of the cable systems that compete with domestic over-the-air broadcasting. Although there are more private satellite operators now (such as Astra and Panamsat), governments—not private enterprises—will continue to launch, operate, and allocate transponder space on the majority of television-carrying satellites for the foreseeable future. And through promotion of domestic programming production, and limits on "foreign" programming content, they can shape importantly many of the viewing choices their national audiences will have.

National economic policies will also play a crucial hand in the evolution of twenty-first-century television. The hard-fought struggle right now over standards for high-definition television (HDTV) is only one of a dozen issues that represent thousands of jobs and billions of dollars for the winners. In the post–cold war era, with economics as the new centerpiece for competitive national relations, few governments will treat television in isolation. The issues of who produces the new technology, who owns the broadcast systems and programming, and what standards will be accepted are as important today as the once obscure issues of rail track width or electrical voltage standards seemed a century ago—with as economically sizable implications. Americans who blithely imagine that global television will emerge as part of a Ricardian world of open trade and free competition do so at their own peril.[10]

WHAT ARE THE ECONOMICS OF GLOBAL TELEVISION?

If income levels and government policies are acting as crucial forces shaping the environment for global television, what are the economics of that system itself, especially as it emerges from its history of government monopoly in many countries? The standard textbook, Bruce Owen and Steven Wildman's *Video Economics*, offers a trio of important, if economically elementary, points that the apostle as well as the critic of global television need to keep in mind:

1. The first and most serious mistake that an analyst of the television industry can make is to assume that . . . broadcasters are in the business to broadcast programming. They are not. Broadcasters are in the business of producing audiences.

2.   It is often said that television stations seek the largest possible audiences, but this is an oversimplification. Advertisers are interested not merely in the size of an audience but in its characteristics . . . the age, sex, and income composition of the audience. . . . Some audiences are more valuable than others.

3.   A television station may be able to increase its audience only at a prohibitive program cost. . . . Although it is true that stations are interested in achieving as large an audience as possible for any given program expenditure, they do not seek to obtain an indefinitely large audience regardless of the cost.[11]

Although Owen and Wildman here are discussing the highly commercial American television market, the points they make—as we shall see—are crucial to understanding how global television is likely to evolve. To do so, first we must grasp the organizational needs of a new global system, including its chief economic institutions.

Structurally, any television system—global or national—consists of four distinct elements. First, there must be a *delivery system*—designated over-the-air frequencies, and/or a satellite or cable network—that can carry an electronic signal from point of origin to a television screen. Second, a *programming system* must exist—a network, an independent over-the-air or cable channel, or a satellite broadcaster capable of organizing programming and ensuring its placement on the delivery system. Third, a *production or creative system*—whether linked to or independent of the broadcast system—must conceive and create the programming (or organize the news or arrange for sports coverage) for the broadcast system to carry. Finally, there must be a *financial payments system* underwriting all this—through advertising, viewer fees, or a tax of some sort—to allow the various systems, directly or indirectly, to operate.

From the early 1950s, when television began, up through the late 1970s, these four elements were provided at the national, not global, level. Governments (again, excepting the United States) generally authorized a single broadcast entity to organize, program, deliver, and financially operate single-nation, over-the-air television systems.

These national systems, though, even at their height, were often part of a very rudimentary precursor of what is today talked about as global television. As early as the mid-1950s, modest amounts of programming were purchased from other countries (the BBC sold its shows to Australia, Canada, and New Zealand, for example) and there was some international exchange of news footage, sports events, and so on. (In Europe, public broadcasters cooperatively exchanged news footage among themselves through the European Broadcast Union.) But all of this was done within a national context, and the delivery of broadcast material between nations was done by sending videotape or film via mail or courier. (In the trade, the delivery was called "bicycling," hinting at its simple origins.)

However small and technologically primitive by modern standards, international sale and exchange of finished programming and raw news footage laid a crucial foundation for the modern possibility of global television—a rudimentary international television market. By the 1960s, activity in the market began to pick up. Hollywood—with fifty years' experience exporting motion picture to foreign theaters—began to discover the foreign television market. It began by selling movies to it, then gradually adding American television series. Targeted primarily at English-speaking markets, by the late 1960s, such sales gradually grew to include continental Europe, Latin America, and the remaining parts of the non-Communist world. (Most American travelers in the period can still recall the surprise of seeing *Bonanza* dubbed into German or *I Love Lucy* into Italian on their hotel television screens.)

In retrospect, these American program exports weren't much of a surprise, at least not economically. Government broadcasters around the world operated with limited revenues and saw the purchase of American programming as a cost-saving measure when compared to their own original domestic program production.

But what made American programming so comparatively cheap? Economically, it reflected two crucial concepts. The first, "sunk costs," applies to the seller. The programming that Hollywood offered in the international market had generally already been produced, shown, and paid for in the American market. In television, because new programming almost always is preferred by audiences to reruns, the economic value of such "old" programming plummets in its originating market. (It is not without value—popular series can earn lucrative residual revenues as reruns—but profit-maximizing producers generally move on to creating "new" programming to earn greater revenues, and profits, domestically.) This leaves a secondary, foreign market, where the program has not been shown before. But here we can see a second concept at work: the wide disparity in income levels and the government dominance of broadcasting historically have shaped the buyer's end of this international programming market into a set of monopsonies.

Program producers sell a product—a single program or series, usually divided into half-hour or hour-long segments, or a movie—to a broadcaster, who in turn shows it to his audience. Ideally, from the seller's end, the program is sold to multiple broadcasters, each delivering (in theory) a spatially separate national audience.

The most striking feature of the broadcasters who serve these distinct audiences is the ongoing variation in the price they will pay for programming, even today. Table 2.2 (see pages 22–23), drawn from a 1993 industry study, shows the average price range a program producer can expect, selling a single, thirty-minute program to various broadcasters around the world. (Certain factors, such as popularity of the show, whether it's part of a series, what else the producer is offering, and so on, can all affect the actual price paid; the table represents the range the producer can reasonably expect.)

Note that selling a program to a U.S. network yields the producer as much as $2,000,000, while selling the same program to a French broadcaster nets between $8,000 and $60,000, and selling it to a Chilean network brings in as little as $1,000.

What is immediately clear is that, while the global market for programming sold to multiple domestic broadcasters may be extensive (that is, covering a very large number of separate markets), the value of those broadcast markets varies enormously. Selling to just half a dozen of them, out of more than two hundred worldwide, will produce more than 83 percent of all the potential income globally available.[12]

Why is this so? One obvious factor, of course, is a market's size: smaller markets, with fewer people, promise lower revenues than larger ones—other factors being equal. But the table itself shows that other factors aren't equal. As mentioned earlier, there is wide variation in personal income among these countries, irrespective of size. Thus, in Africa, Asia, Latin America, and Eastern Europe, lower per capita incomes—and substantially fewer television sets (hence smaller audiences)—not total population, account for much of the low price levels paid for programming.

But income—and per capita television sets—do not fully explain the difference either. As the table indicates, Western Europe, Canada, and Japan all have high per capita incomes; even adjusting for audience size doesn't explain why a program's value in the United States is four to six times greater per viewer than in other advanced industrial countries.

In the United States—which has relatively high average incomes, competition among networks and stations, and an advertising-based revenue stream—program producers earn high gross revenues. But in countries with dual public/private systems that have similarly high incomes, though, producers clearly do not have the ability to generate similar revenues. (When programs are sold into countries with a traditionally straightforward television monopoly, little or no advertising, and low average personal incomes, producers' sales revenue plummets.) Why does a continuing government presence in these television markets apparently hold down programmer income?

The television markets of the advanced industrial countries today (other than the United States) are a public/private mix—in which government channels still capture the largest audience share collectively, and in which the amount of advertising carried on both public and private channels is strictly regulated. From the 1950s through the 1970s, their governments operated television monopolies that had no particular reason to bid up the price of programming they purchased, nor to worry particularly about audience acceptance (and hence audience size) for the programs they broadcast. Viewers either watched, or they didn't, and program purchase prices stayed low.

The historic fact of government monopoly alone does not explain why in the dual public/private systems of industrialized nations today, programmer income is still lower than in the United States. After all, deregulation has existed long enough to approximate competitive, U.S.-style markets—or has it?

The reality is that, in these dual systems, in which the public broadcaster still relies for much of its income on license fees as well as advertising, an indirect cap is placed on private broadcasters' advertising income. By dividing the market between public and private channels, with the public channels capturing substantial license income, these public channels hold advertising rates below the level a private-only market would have. This in turn lowers the income private channels are able to spend on programming, whether imported or domestic.

Table 2.3 (see pages 24–26) helps illustrate the point more clearly. A 1991 survey of television advertising spending globally shows the variation in spending, both gross and per capita, among nations. In the United States, television advertising approached $30 billion annually, with per capita advertising expenditures at nearly $120. Japan, with the oldest dual public/private system (dating back to the American Occupation), has the second highest overall spending ($16 billion) and per capita expenditure ($101). In Western Europe, where private channels basically date only from the late 1970s and early 1980s, total television advertising roughly equals Japan's (at $17.4 billion), but is spread across a population nearly three times larger. Per capita spending on advertising, as a consequence, is significantly lower—at $40, barely a third that of the United States and Japan.

In Europe, lower per capita advertising spending levels are compensated for, at least with public broadcasters, through their license

TABLE 2.2
GLOBAL TV PROGRAM PRICES
(Range Paid per Half-Hour Program in International Trade)

REGION/COUNTRY		LOW $	HIGH $
NORTH AMERICA			
Canada	CBC English	12,000	60,000
	CTV	10,000	60,000
United States	Main network	100,000	2,000,000
	Pay cable	50,000	1,250,000
	Basic cable	5,000	250,000
	PBS network	50,000	250,000
	Syndication	30,000	100,000
CENTRAL & SOUTH AMERICA			
Argentina		1,500	5,000
Brazil		2,500	12,000
Mexico		2,500	10,000
Venezuela		5,000	7,000
WESTERN EUROPE			
France		6,000	60,000
Germany		15,000	80,000
Italy		8,000	60,000
Spain		7,000	35,000
Sweden		2,500	6,500
Switzerland		2,500	5,000
United Kingdom	BBC/ITV	20,000	100,000
	Channel 4	15,000	70,000
	Satellite	1,000	70,000
	Cable	2,000	4,000
EASTERN EUROPE			
Hungary		800	1,000
Poland		750	1,500
Romania		700	1,000
Former Soviet Union		1,000	5,000

REGION/COUNTRY		LOW $	HIGH $
ASIA & THE FAR EAST			
China		1,000	2,000
India		1,000	1,500
Indonesia		700	1,200
Japan	NHK	10,000	40,000
	Commercial	15,000	150,000
Philippines		1,000	1,700
OCEANIA			
Australia	ABC	9,000	45,000
	Commercial	20,000	100,000
MIDDLE EAST			
Iran		750	1,500
Iraq*		800	1,000
Israel		500	1,350
Kuwait		1,000	1,200
Saudi Arabia		1,500	2,000
AFRICA			
Egypt		1,000	1,200
Ethiopia		200	600
Kenya		200	750
Morocco		300	500
Nigeria		1,500	3,000
South Africa		2,000	7,000
CARIBBEAN			
Cuba		400	450

* Prices which could be commanded during normal times.
Source: Adapted from "Global Program Price Guide," Television Business International, May 1993, p. 76.

TABLE 2.3
WORLDWIDE TELEVISION ADVERTISING EXPENDITURES

REGION/COUNTRY	POPULATION (MILLIONS)	1991 ADVERTISING EXPORTS (US$ MILLIONS)	ADVERTISING EXPORTS PER CAPITA (US$)	FORECAST 1992 ADVERTISING EXPORTS (US$ MILLIONS)	FORECAST REAL GROWTH, 1992 v. 1991 (%)	FORECAST REAL GROWTH, 1993 v. 1992 (%)
AFRICA	77.6	311	4.0	337	8.3	6.4
South Africa[1]	35.3	311	8.8	337	8.3	6.4
ASIA/PACIFIC	2,493.7	16,988	6.8	17,763	4.6	4.3
Australia[1]	17.1	1,257	73.5	1,231	-2.1	-0.7
China[2]	1,135.0	88	0.1	107	21.4	21.3
India[1]	827.1	134	0.2	149	11.2	5.7
Japan[3]	123.5	12,466	100.9	12,778	2.5	2.4
Philippines[4]	61.5	126	2.0	141	11.8	17.5
South Korea[4]	42.8	880	20.6	1,051	19.4	9.9
EUROPE	432.8	17,435	40.3	18,249	4.7	4.2
France[1]	56.4	2,369	42.0	2,393	1.0	1.4
Germany	77.6	2,233	28.8	2,548	14.1	7.3
Italy	57.7	3,608	62.5	3,767	4.4	3.3

REGION/COUNTRY	POPULATION (MILLIONS)	1991 ADVERTISING EXPORTS (US$ MILLIONS)	ADVERTISING EXPORTS PER CAPITA (US$)	FORECAST 1992 ADVERTISING EXPORTS (US$ MILLIONS)	FORECAST REAL GROWTH, 1992 v. 1991 (%)	FORECAST REAL GROWTH, 1993 v. 1992 (%)
EUROPE (Continued)						
Spain	39.0	2,466	63.2	2,399	-2.7	-0.2
Switzerland	6.7	153	22.8	153	0.1	2.8
United Kingdom[3]	57.4	4,176	72.8	4,264	2.1	3.7
LATIN AMERICA/ CARIBBEAN	155.6	1,846	11.9	2,110	14.3	8.6
Argentina[3]	[32.3]	[251]	[7.8]	—	—	—
Brazil[3]	[150.2]	[1,826]	[12.2]	—	—	—
Mexico[1]	86.2	800	9.3	882	10.2	8.1
Venezuela[1]	19.7	335	17.0	402	20	25.0
MIDDLE EAST						
Israel[5]	[4.6]	[20]	[4.3]	—	—	—
Saudi Arabia[5]	[14.9]	[50]	[3.4]	—	—	—

TABLE 2.3 (Continued)
WORLDWIDE TELEVISION ADVERTISING EXPENDITURES

REGION/COUNTRY	POPULATION (MILLIONS)	1991 ADVERTISING EXPORTS (US$ MILLIONS)	ADVERTISING EXPORTS PER CAPITA (US$)	FORECAST 1992 ADVERTISING EXPORTS (US$ MILLIONS)	FORECAST REAL GROWTH, 1992 v. 1991 (%)	FORECAST REAL GROWTH, 1993 v. 1992 (%)
NORTH AMERICA	276.5	30,949	111.9	30,689	-0.8	0.5
Canada	26.5	1,369	51.7	1,435	4.8	4.4
United States[3]	250.0	29,580	118.3	29,255	-1.1	0.3

[1] Agency commission included in expenditure totals, production costs excluded.
[2] China and countries without a footnote have both production costs and agency commission excluded from expenditure totals.
[3] Both production costs and agency commission included in expenditure totals.
[4] Production costs details not given, agency commission included.
[5] Neither production costs nor agency commission details are given.

Note: All the Zenith figures in the 1991 expenditure column are for 1991, whereas all the Starch INRA Hooper figures in the same column are for 1990 only. For this reason the latter are not included in the region totals. Countries listed are a representative sample for each region, not a complete breakdown of region figures.

Sources: The figures in this table have been taken from two worldwide reports of national population and advertising expenditure data. Zenith Media Worldwide figures are without brackets and Starch INRA Hooper figures are in brackets.

fees. In 1991, gross West European license fees totaled nearly $12.9 billion—at a time when advertising revenues continue to grow as a percentage of broadcasters' total income. Moreover, although private competition grew tremendously in the 1980s, license fees had risen steadily (both in nominal and real terms) throughout the period, allowing the public systems to hold their advertising rates below what they would have been had the systems' revenues been purely advertising-based.[13] This downward pressure on advertising rates by the public systems in turn placed an upward cap on the rates the private competition could charge, since the public systems still held major audience share.

Table 2.3 also shows clearly the role that advertising plays in television outside the United States, Europe, and Japan—a crucial factor in any discussion of the possibilities for global television's success. Note how in Asia, for example, Japan and Australia (with 6 percent of the region's population) account for over 80 percent of television advertising spending. Or, how all of Latin America, with a population 50 percent larger than the United States, amounts to 6 percent of the U.S. television advertising revenues. Or, most strikingly, how Middle East advertising dollars total barely $100 million, or how African television advertising spending (apart from South Africa) is virtually nil.

As we shall see, the size of the advertising market outside the industrialized West, Japan, and Australia is a minor fraction of the monies spent inside the world's industrial core. While deregulation is bringing rapid growth to many of these markets, the bases from which they start often are no larger than some midsized metropolitan television advertising markets in the United States. Would-be global broadcasters are by no means wholly dependent on advertising alone for potential revenues, but advertising is a major part of their strategy for profitability. Thus, once again, we are brought back to the realization of the role income and government policy—not just toward television, but in economic growth—will play in the future for global television. Far from being a matter simply of technology driving a global future, we are forced to wrestle with some of the oldest questions the world has faced.

3

How Global Television Is Redefining Our Notions of Property

Although the birth of global television is most often attributed to new technologies, its origins rest more accurately in a legal and regulatory shift that took root in the 1960s. However, it was not until the Reagan/Thatcher era that the public took notice of the consequences; hence, the change sometimes has been attributed to the triumph of an aggressive new conservatism at the executive level. In fact, the "communications revolution" had been percolating since the late 1960s within the broadcast regulatory community—foremost, ironically, in the world's most competitive television market.

The First Rounds of Change

As early as the presidency of John F. Kennedy, academics, FCC economists, and congressional staff had begun looking closely at the FCC's network regulatory model—and compared it highly disadvantageously to models of competitive markets. The critical first step toward possible television "deregulation," however, didn't come until the waning days of the administration of Lyndon B. Johnson. A presidential task force headed by Eugene Rostow concluded that federal broadcast regulation had become "over-extensive," and acted "as a constraint on competition" in markets that lacked "natural monopoly" characteristics. But with public attention focused on the Vietnam War and domestic upheaval, few (apart from specialists) took note of the report or the underlying debates.

A new push came from Richard Nixon's White House Office of Telecommunications Policy. Clay Whitehead, the director and a strong market advocate, pushed through the Nixon administration's "Open Skies" policy, forcing the FCC to support a competitive domestic satellite industry, rather than let it slip under the control of the Bell system—a crucial first step, it turned out, in launching satellite television broadcasting. He also pressed for reform of the tiny cable television industry (which the FCC had until then virtually ignored), as well as for extensive telephone service deregulation.

By the time Jimmy Carter entered office, Congress joined the White House in pressing further "deregulation"—not only of broadcasting, but of telephones, airlines, trucking, rail, and financial services. In broadcasting, the trend was encouraged by a handful of private foundations, such as the Ford Foundation and the Markle Foundation, that had sponsored extensive research, organized conferences, and generally pressed, quietly but effectively, for a new look at the issue of public regulation. The result, as Bruce Owen and Steven Wildman observe, was dramatic: "As more and more economists and legal scholars became interested in broadcast regulation and as the flow of published research increased, the perceived legitimacy of the FCC's policies, and worse, its motives, waned." [1]

In Europe, a similar process—starting from the different experience of government monopoly, rather than regulation—got under way. Beginning in the 1970s, many governments began to reassess the practice of *broadcast monopoly*. For a host of reasons, they began to implement changes in the organization of their television broadcast systems.

Most commonly, European governments did two things. First, they introduced *competitive* broadcasting, by licensing private owners to operate stations that opened up the range of choice available to viewers. Second, they required of their own government networks increasing *commercialization*, which included carrying advertising, greater diversity in their programming, audience research, and so on, making the networks closer to private broadcasters. (In some cases, along with licensing new private channels, they increased the number of government channels, all subject to commercialization.)

For Europe, the consequences were both swift and significant. From the mid-1970s to the mid-1980s, the number of channels in Western Europe more than doubled, to 75; by 1990, the number was 117, and it will approach 150 by the mid-1990s. Overwhelmingly, competition was the key factor in this growth. With most of the channels launched privately, by 1989 these new private channels exceeded the number under public management. With this expansion of channels (and a lengthening of on-air time), the number of hours broadcast across Europe likewise exploded. In 1980, approximately 120,000 hours were being broadcast annually; by 1990, the number exceeded 400,000; and by the end of this year, according to some estimates, it may reach 600,000.[2]

Thus, as broadcast monopolies lost their control, whether through competition or commercialization, viewer choice increased, and total viewing hours, advertising revenue, and demand for programming all rose as well. As we shall see, however, neither demand nor supply is perfectly (or even very) elastic, which holds powerful implications for the future of global television.

THE SECOND ROUND OF CHANGE

By the 1980s, a second round of changes followed—sparked by a combination of new technology, falling costs, and further spread of the new theories of government regulation. The technological change pivoted on improved satellite capabilities, miniaturization of ground receiving equipment, and the opportunities offered by cable. The cost reductions were a consequence of the technological changes, and came in three separate areas simultaneously.

First, more and improved satellites lowered the cost of satellite transmission (and expanded coverage area). This encouraged yet further use by over-the-air national broadcasters, who used satellite (instead of phone lines) to move programming to affiliates and remote transmitters, as well as international locations. Second, the reduced size of receiving dishes suddenly made "home dishes" available to consumers as well as corporations—thereby effectively extending the economic "market" for satellite transmission into the home. Third, cable operators, who competed for the same "home" market, could now use satellite to distribute their own increased programming at lower cost. In turn, initial financial successes gave cable operators lower marginal costs per viewer, and hence much larger operating profits. Those profits gave them more ability to compete against both traditional over-the-air broadcasting and their would-be satellite-to-home competitors.

As a consequence, the technological breakthroughs of the 1980s spawned a major increase in satellite use for transmission and rebroadcast. In turn, in the United States and Europe, a three-way battle was started among the new direct-to-home (DTH) satellite systems, the cable operators, and the old over-the-air broadcasters for economic control of the "home" viewer market.

While the deregulation debate had a less visible impact outside the United States and Western Europe during most of the 1980s, it nonetheless, for indirect reasons, began to exert itself in many countries, especially in the developing and Communist worlds.

By the 1980s, much of the Third World was mired in the trillion-dollar-plus "global debt crisis," brought about by the OPEC price hikes and free-for-all petro-dollar recycling of the 1970s. Burdened with gigantic debts and little prospect of paying them off, many of these countries found themselves actively "encouraged" by Western banks and multinational lenders, such as the International Monetary Fund and World Bank, to sell off state-owned assets, including broadcasting facilities and rights. As a result, by the end of the decade, one saw—particularly in Latin America and East Asia—a rapid surge of interest in the creation of viable private competition with public television along European lines, including cable, satellite, and over-the-air alternatives to the traditional government monopolies.

Meanwhile, of course, the Gorbachev revolution was bringing sweeping change to the Communist world. With the fall of the Berlin Wall, and then Gorbachev himself, the newly post-Communist countries of Eastern Europe and the Commonwealth of Independent States found themselves debating the future of broadcasting for their 400 million television viewers. Since Communism's collapse, no former Soviet Bloc state broadcaster has actually yet gone out of business (as with most of the rest of the world), but most of the countries are moving to make their broadcast authorities into semiautonomous agencies, and to allow private channel competition, including cable and satellite broadcasting.

The scope of these changes—both technological and political—and their sweep across such an extensive part of the planet's population are what has seemed to set the stage for global broadcasting. Just as national competitors have found the new technologies opening up whole new modes of national broadcast, the change in the regulatory environment in so many countries has opened up the application of those technologies to international—and indeed, seemingly global—opportunities. By the end of the 1980s, it was thus not surprising to find many who spoke of global television as just around the corner.

CREATING NEW PROPERTY AND WEALTH — AND THE IMPLICATIONS FOR PUBLIC POLICY

In much of the late-1980s talk about global villages, the pervasive focus was on the technological features of the decade's changes (and falling costs)—the wizardry of satellites, the novelty of home satellite dishes, the abundance of channels (if not always variety) offered by cable. Lost, to the general public at least, were issues being raised by the so-called regulatory revolution that has paralleled the technological developments, and in many ways made them feasible.

Yet the regulatory shift of the past two decades—first in the United States, then Europe, and now spreading around the world—contains in it crucial questions, the answers to which will shape the economic market for global television as profoundly as any of the technological achievements to date. At play are not only issues of national sovereignty, but of property and ownership interests that belie the common shibboleth of the television viewer—in no matter what country—as nothing more than a "consumer" of television programming (and the advertised products which sponsor it). As already seen, governments are not "abandoning" their television markets to private interests, and they will play crucial, multiple roles for years to come. Understanding their philosophically appropriate roles is one of the crucial tests of the next period.

The term "regulatory revolution" in fact points only inexactly, and rather poorly, at what has been going on in recent years—a process of even more fundamental change lies beneath the phrase. Milton Mueller, in a recent *Gannett Center Journal* article, has helpfully underscored both that "revolution" and its antecedents, which to date have remained the realm of specialists:

> In every arena touched by new technologies of telecommunications, property relations and ownership controls are being rapidly transformed and neither "deregulation" nor "the transition from monopoly to competition" touch on the real significance of events. . . . What makes these changes truly revolutionary is that they are extending the capitalist mode of economic organization into parts of the economy which have been exempt from it for centuries. Property and exchange relations are being established where none existed before.[3]

How do these concerns relate to the emergence of global television? As noted, far from the simple model of the public as passive viewers or consumers of television—whose only desire is to maximize choice among programming alternatives—other quite important questions of public policy and the public interest are at play.

Consider the issue of satellite, rocket, and launch-related technologies as one example. Developed during the cold war in just a handful of countries (led by the United States and Soviet Union), they were primarily military technologies and were pursued at public

expense. The question now is: Who should share as economic benefi-
ciaries today and in the future, as private broadcasters turn increasingly to these technologies for delivery of their programming? Have
the costs allocated historically by NASA to Intelsat, and in turn by
Intelsat to government (and now private) users fully reflected the
underlying public investment? How should U.S. policymakers—since
the United States served as principal supplier and launcher of satellites
in the past—view newly emergent competition from European,
Japanese, and now Russian, Chinese, and Third-World alternatives?
Particularly given the low costs of the Russian and Chinese launch services, should the United States—following strictly comparative advantage rules—abandon the low end of its telecommunications launch
capacity (apart from military needs) as it has given way on other high-
tech issues such as computer and chip manufacturing?

How is the public interest represented in the process of international spectrum allocation, an arrangement essential to broadcast via
satellite? Historically, such allocation has been considered an issue of a
"public good" handled by a multinational public agency, the International Telecommunications Union (ITU). But with the explosion in
satellite numbers (over 2,000 are now already in orbit, with 125 devoted
just to television relay),[4] the old "first-come, first-served" rule has been
forced to give way to a much more complex regime of allocation. That
system in turn has been complicated by the launch of private satellites
such as Astra and Panamsat, and raises pressing questions—not only
about competing interests among nations, but between public and private broadcasters and satellite operators—that won't just go away.[5]

Cable raises its own set of issues, as an alternative to both terrestrial over-the-air and satellite transmission. Historically, television
developed nationally as a "free," over-the-air system (paid for either by
advertisers or, in certain government monopoly systems, by viewer
fees). Cable, in bypassing that transmission system, creates vital and
contentious issues of payment and ownership questions of its own.
Because it charges viewers for access (both on a monthly basis, and
secondly through pay-per-view), it is transforming seemingly "free"
public access into a decidedly private, and for-profit, alternative.
Congress has already moved to partly reregulate the U.S. cable industry after a decade of rapidly rising charges to viewers. The issue of paying several hundred dollars per year, as a precedent for access to
"global" television, particularly in poor countries, where the majority
of the world's population still lives, in turn raises some of the most
fundamental questions about equality imaginable—all, at this point,
philosophically and practically unresolved.

The cable issue in the future, moreover, will likely grow even more highly charged, as first the United States, and then other advanced industrial nations, move toward the widely discussed "fiber-optics highway" option. To the degree that private cable systems supplant previously publicly controlled or regulated public airwaves, what is the public interest in maintaining public control over these private operators? Although there is competition to win new territories, once in place, cable systems operate as "natural monopolies" without direct competition. In the United States, over 60 percent of television households pay for cable (in the Benelux countries and Switzerland, the percentage is even higher); are these operators to be left solely to "market" regulation? And with cost estimates of proposed fiber-optics highways running into the hundreds of billions of dollars just for the United States, who should control them—let alone pay for their creation? The existing cable operators? The phone companies? Taxpayers? Cable subscribers?

Who should own the newly created wealth opportunities resulting from deregulation and privatization of what were once public assets? Should new competitors be helped against older, established players, to make the markets more vibrant, or should the markets alone determine outcome? Should parts of these new systems be reserved for public broadcasters forever? What responsibilities should such public broadcasters have, if not merely the economic one to turn a profit? What programming ought not be allowed on television? And—especially in an age that emphasizes international competition—what, if any limits, ought to be placed on ownership of television assets by foreign individuals and corporations?

Eli Noam has noted, for example, that in the European media reforms of the 1980s, although governments stepped sharply away from public broadcast monopolies, the awarding of private licenses was far from freely competitive. In moving from public monopoly, television's evolution became mired in the current stage, which Noam calls dryly the era of "Television of Privilege."[6] In it, dominant political parties routinely have awarded those licenses to political allies, who in turn have often proved less than anxious to see further opening of the domestic television market. And certainly politics is far from absent in the fierce debates about the future of American television, with competing networks, producers, cable companies, satellite operators, and telephone companies all jockeying for advantage in the political arena. What one can fairly conclude is that the media future is still deeply embedded not only in the mundane world of political spoils, but in a less-understood debate about the very nature of property itself, and who will gain by its control. Without some sort of coherent debate about these issues—reaching well beyond the customary conversations about channel growth and viewer opportunity—there is little chance of a public understanding about just what is at stake in terms of property in the debate over global television.

4

THE LAYERS OF THE EMERGING GLOBAL MARKET

When Americans talk or read about global television, the first subject that usually comes up these days is CNN International. Now
visible in more than 200 countries, it seems the very model for what
commonly seems to be meant by global television. In fact, it is only
one part of a complex market for single-source, satellite-based,
transnational broadcasting.

Since CNNI's creation eight years ago, Ted Turner's Atlanta-based
network has been joined globally by the BBC's World Service
Television and by MTV's European, Latin American, and Asian efforts.
On a regional basis, it has been joined by Rupert Murdoch's Sky News
and the EBU's Euronews in Europe; Star TV (recently acquired by
Murdoch) and TVB-International in Asia; the Middle East Broadcast
Center in the Arab world; Televisa's Eco and NBC's Spanish-language
service in Latin America; and South Africa's M-Net in Africa. In addi-
tion, there is almost daily talk of new global or regional satellite-based
competitors, ranging from Japan's NHK to French-language broadcasting directed at Francophone Africa.

With so much apparent activity in the global television field—and
new entrants seemingly anxious to enter—it's helpful to distinguish
at least three separate concepts that often intermingle when global
television is discussed.

The first is *international television*, the oldest of the three categories, which suggests simply the transfer of television programming
(or program license) through sale or barter, from one country to another or others. This particular form of trade dates back to the mid-1950s,
and was discussed in Chapter 2.

Second is the idea of *multinational television*, which suggests a more
kaleidoscopic set of relations that includes much wider program transfer,

coproduction of programming, regional (rather than national) broadcasting, and transnational ownership of broadcasting and production
facilities. For the most part, this newer form began in the 1980s, with the
technological and regulatory changes that characterized the decade.

Finally, there is the *global television* of the 1990s, with an expansive multinationalism that promises to make all, or at least a great portion, of the planet's television audience available to a set of individual
broadcasters.[1] It certainly includes many of the features of multinational television, but in scope vastly transcends the regional ambitions
of multinationalism.

Global television may be the topic of the hour, but of the three
categories, international television is by far the largest in economic
terms. Beginning in the 1950s, America built on its experience in theatrical motion picture exports by selling movies to foreign broadcasters. In turn, European, Japanese, and smaller markets sought export
markets for their own motion picture industries.[2] By the early 1960s,
this process gradually began to include trade in television programs,
particularly of domestically popular American television series.

From its inception forty years ago, however, this international
trade in programming has been far from global as we commonly use
the term. Even today, it remains overwhelmingly a bilateral, trans-
Atlantic affair, in economic terms. Second, it has been a decidedly
one-way trade: measured in dollars, this international market has been
one of Europeans buying U.S. exports.

International trade data show this concentration and flow pattern quite clearly. In 1989, for example, total world exports of television
programming amounted to $2.4 billion. Of that trade, U.S. exports
accounted for 71 percent of the total. Appetite for those U.S. exports,
in turn, was similarly concentrated: Western Europe imported three-
quarters of them, with a price tag of $1.3 billion. (By comparison, U.S.
imports of foreign programming amounted to barely $160 million, less
than 2 percent of U.S. programming hours.)

Ignoring the United States and Europe as television program
importers, the remaining 170 or so nations of the world, with 88 percent of the earth's population, made less than $700 million in inter-
national programming purchases—barely a quarter of the global total.[3]
Or, as one U.S. television executive bluntly put it, "This business is
about as 'global' as a one-way New York-to-London plane ticket is a
trip around the world."[4]

The market figures in Table 4.1 show in greater detail just how this
nominally international television trade has both behaved in recent
years, and is likely to unfold.

TABLE 4.1
ESTIMATED INTERNATIONAL PROGRAM EXPORTS
1987 PROJECTED TO 1995

	1987	1989	1991	1993	1995
EXPORTS ($ millions)					
United States	1,119	1,696	2,096	2,521	3,005
Western European	161	426	660	910	1,175
Other	194	273	393	566	815
TOTAL	1,474	2,395	3,149	3,997	4,995
% OF TOTAL					
United States	76	71	67	63	60
Western Europe	11	18	21	23	24
Others	13	11	12	14	16

U.S. EXPORT MARKET SHARE COMPARED TO OTHER IMPORTS (%)*

	1987	1989	1991	1993	1995
In Western Europe	77	79	78	76	74
Outside Western Europe	75	71	62	60	57

WESTERN EUROPE EXPORT MARKET SHARES COMPARED TO OTHER IMPORTS (%)*

	1987	1989	1991	1993	1995
In United States	68	70	72	73	76
Outside United States	4	10	18	20	24

*Does not include competition from domestic production.

Note: Because of rounding, percents may appear to add up to 101. "Western Europe" includes European Union Countries and Austria, Switzerland, and Scandinavia.

Source: Adapted from Neil Weinstock, U.S. and International Programming (Frost & Sullivan, New York, 1991).

Several things are noteworthy. First, the good news for Hollywood (and U.S. balance-of-payments) is that the international programming market is still expanding rapidly. From 1987 to 1995, chiefly as a result of new European channels, the increase will be from under $1.5 billion to nearly $5 billion—more than a three-fold increase. And as in the past, because it continues to purchase more than half the programming sold internationally, Western Europe still drives that growth as it searches for ways to fill broadcasting hours now available as a result of new channels.

Although the United States has been the chief beneficiary of this explosion in European television (at the beginning of the 1980s, U.S. exports to Europe were under $200 million), future market growth is not without major problems for American studios. Within the overall global growth curve, the U.S. share of total market is declining, even while growing in dollar terms. The growth in exports is shifting from the United States to the countries of Western Europe, which have effectively doubled their market share in the past five years.

This shift—U.S. sales growth dropping below the total market growth, the appearance of a sizable competitive Western European export market—is prompting new growth in what we have defined as the multinational—as distinct from the international—market for television. The implications, as we shall see, reach well beyond the old trans-Atlantic trade.[5]

THE SHIFT TO MULTINATIONAL PROGRAMMING

Multinational broadcasting doesn't by itself imply a leap into a new era of globalism for television. Nor is it simply *replacing* the older international trade. Rather, it is *supplementing* the older form by forging a new category in television trade among nations.

Multinationalism's emergence reflects a tectonic shift in the trans-Atlantic international market. The shift has been caused primarily by two changes in the European television environment: first, the already-examined privatization and commercialization of television itself, and second, the rise of the European Union with its quest for an integrated, continental market.

When competitive broadcasting made viewer choice a reality, European broadcasters discovered that an old shibboleth—that their audiences readily accepted foreign programming—was little more than a myth. Given a choice, viewers now showed a decided preference for original programming in their own language, with characters, plots, and styles that reflected national—rather than Hollywood's—culture.[6]

This discovery, however, presented a challenge to the broadcasters, since the cost of original programming was much higher than purchase of American reruns.

A recent study by the Annenberg Washington Program summarized the cost dilemma facing the new European broadcasters:

> If considered as a single unit, the [European Community] may represent the largest media market in the world. . . . However, Europe's media industry is fragmented by culture, language, taste, and regulation. . . . [consequently] there is no truly pan-European media market, and European media groups are relatively weak.[7]

One significant measure of that market fragmentation, the study noted, is that 85 percent of all European television programming is never transmitted beyond its original national, or linguistic, borders.

For European broadcasters—as channels and viewing hours grew—the question was how to provide domestic programming to relatively small audiences. *Coproduction* and *outside production* became the watchwords of the new multinational approach. By dividing costs and responsibilities through coproduction among production divisions or subsidiaries of two or more broadcasters, often from different countries, program producers could divide the costs, and hence the risks, associated with program production. By using independent producers, rather than the broadcasters themselves, to generate the programming, costs and risks could likewise be reduced for the broadcasters.

Measured in dollar terms, it is easy to see just how significant multinational programming has become. In 1992, coproduction and outside production represented more than $2.8 billion of Western Europe's programming purchases; imports were $2.15 billion. By 1995, the gap will grow—multinational programming will be nearly $5.3 billion, while imports will rise only modestly, to $2.7 billion.

Another measure of the spread of multinational coproduction comes from a survey conducted by the trade journal *Television Business International*, in association with the William Morris Agency. Conducted in late 1989, the survey—which was extensive, but by no means comprehensive—found 78 active coproductions in France, 82 in the United Kingdom, 52 in Germany, 42 in Italy, 61 in the United States, 25 in Canada, and dozens more scattered among the smaller states of Europe.[8]

The mention of sixty-one U.S. coproductions is evidence that the new multinational programming wave is far from an exclusively

European phenomenon. As European television has grown, American producers have reacted to the challenge posed by the multinational alternative, especially since the multinational export trade threatened to become, more accurately, "multi-European" in scope.

A second factor in the U.S. reaction to multinational production has been the fear of foreign quotas on U.S. programming. For years, European cultural critics had denounced the "Hollywoodization" of European cultural life—first through movies, and then through television exports. One of the most powerful arguments against privatizing European television was that more channels would open a floodgate to American sitcoms and melodramas such as *Dallas* and *Dynasty*. The French particularly—personified in Minister of Culture Jack Lang—goaded the European Community into looking carefully at setting restrictive quotas on further imports of U.S. television shows. Ultimately, the threatened "quotas" proved to be so loosely drawn as to be ineffectual, but the warning was heard on both sides of the Atlantic.[9]

Still, a recent U.S. industry study makes clear the implications that Hollywood took from Europe's change of television regimes in the 1980s:

> U.S-based and other foreign producers who would sell their teleproductions in the Europe of the 1990s must increasingly: a) engage in coproductions with the Europeans; b) produce their own shows partly in Europe; and, c) help distribute European productions elsewhere, in order to maintain access to their European markets. . . .
>
> Large U.S. producers, eager to extend their sales successes in Europe, can [also] be expected to cooperate with Europeans to produce shows saleable in the U.S., thus changing the long tradition of ratings disasters for foreign shows on U.S. TV. Only those European producers willing and able to work closely with U.S. partners and buyers will achieve this export success.[10]

The result is that multinational programming now is growing quickly—indeed, quite surprisingly so. The consulting firm Booz Allen & Hamilton, examining the coproduction field, estimates that it is expanding at the rate of 30 to 40 percent per annum, heavily concentrated in the cost-intensive film-for-television, drama, and miniseries segments of the industry. Sampling fifty coproductions, totalling 275 hours of broadcast time, Booz Allen found that American producers were responding to the multi-European coproduction by increasing their own participation. While inter-European coproductions account-ed for 40 percent of their sample, European-United States deals were close behind at 34 percent.[11]

THE IMPACT ON GLOBALIZATION

Why are the markets in international and multinational production and trade important to the prospects for global television? First, because their form—that is, their heavy reliance on the European and American markets—lets us see once again how important income is in shaping television markets. The affluence of Europe and the United States has meant that, for the past forty years, the international trade has really been primarily a bilateral, trans-Atlantic trade in fact.

Second, because focusing on multinational programming can also let us see that the new technology and regulatory environment of the 1980s—which supporters cite as laying the ground for globalism—is spawning a process decidedly more complex.

As European broadcasters discovered in the 1980s, the demand for foreign programming—once a decently produced alternative is available—is substantially less than they had imagined, and less than critics of Hollywoodization had so vocally feared. This represents no small challenge to proponents of a global television future, because it suggests that rather than serving to unify separate national markets, the changes of the 1980s are actually strengthening national broad-cast systems, even as the number of broadcasters per country grows.

Indeed, too much focus on international and multinational mar-kets can lead us astray from a central fact almost never underscored in the discussion of globalizing television: the vast majority of program-ming is produced, aired, and remains in a single country. In the United States, of course, this has always been true: barely 2 percent of pro-gram hours broadcast come from overseas, mainly British imports. But the same has always been true of the lucrative Japanese market as well, where barely 5 percent of programming is imported. And as noted earlier, when the EC set out to consider quotas on foreign (that is, U.S. television) imports, it in fact discovered—after a decade of channel and broadcast hour proliferation—that 85 percent of all broadcast hours in Western Europe are conceived, produced, aired in—and never leave—their country of origin.

These conclusions aren't limited to the huge trans-Atlantic market, either. If we look at aggregate programming expenditures globally, we are likewise led—contrary to the image of an emerging globalism—to the same conclusion. In comparison to the $2.4 billion trade in international programming, for example, the sum of spending by broadcasters on their domestic programming is more than $70 billion, measured in dollars. (If measured in purchasing power parity, the number exceeds $80 billion a year.)[12]

Spending isn't the only measure of domestic programming's enduring—and resilient—power. It shows itself even more clearly in what is actually aired on television systems around the world. A recent survey of television viewing in more than sixty countries found that domestic shows overwhelmingly dominate primetime, leading its authors to the following conclusion:

> Neither the worldwide onslaught of US programming on indigenous TV stations feared by some, nor the predictions of high revenues derived from exports to "liberated" markets anticipated by others, have materialized. . . .
>
> The television production industries of an ever-increasing number of countries are reaching maturity, and . . . the origins of top-rated programs in primetime are overwhelmingly domestic. Local production industries are increasingly able to cater to national tastes, and indigenous audiences are now less tolerant of subtitled or dubbed versions of foreign imports. . . . Primetime slots that used to ensure high returns to US producers and distributors 10–15 years ago are now virtually a no-go area. In absolute terms, the volume of imports might have increased, but they are used to fill the off-peak period of an ever-extending schedule.[13]

The report goes on to underline several significant trends that run directly counter to the notion of technology leading in lock-step to simple globalization. First, is the allure of national prestige coupled with the opportunity for domestic profits: most television stations, having invested heavily in them, now regard indigenous productions as "flagship" programming, and now schedule it—not imports—in prime time. Second—and of significant import for would-be global broadcasters—television systems with a small programming budget tend increasingly to concentrate on news/public affairs magazines rather than more expensive drama, having discovered (as U.S. networks did a decade ago) that news can be a popular and profitable product. Third—also significant to global news hopefuls—in general, publicly owned stations tend to heavily favor news- and information-based programming in prime time, and seem to be winning large audiences for it, even against entertainment competition scheduled by private competitors. Fourth, in developing countries, although many still import heavily, domestic programming is making dramatic strides. For example, while Indonesia and Singapore still import heavily, the percentages are declining, and in countries such as Taiwan, South Korea, and Venezuela, broadcasters now rely primarily on domestic production.

In short, on the eve of a presumed new global era for television, domestic—not international, or even regional—broadcasting is surprisingly powerful, if measured in terms of programming. The changes brought by the 1980s may have made foreign programming more technologically available, but the evidence is that actual use of such programming in the schedules of most broadcasters is weakening, especially in the all-important prime-time hours.

By itself, this doesn't refute the idea that a world of more homogenous programming will emerge. It does, however, underscore why industry figures such as Silvio Berlusconi are so cautious about how quickly or completely it will happen. Coupled with the fact that national public broadcasters remain a powerful force, with large audiences, and a strong interest in preserving not only their own roles, but an identifiable national television culture that justifies those roles, the size of domestic programming is of no small significance.

But are there other factors driving global television? Are the precedents of international and multinational trade irrelevant to a global model? Are Berlusconi's doubts only those of a business competitor without his own global network? And can national broadcasters—public or private—hope to compete with the glamorous idea of global alternatives? To examine those questions, we need to examine how the idea of global broadcasting itself arose in the last few years.

5

THE RISE OF GLOBAL BROADCASTING—AND THE MARKETS FOR INTERNATIONAL NEWS

In one sense, the inauguration of global television can fairly be attributed to one man—Ted Turner. In 1985, his vision of a global system of twenty-four-hour news, modeled on CNN's success domestically, led him to launch CNN International, barely five years after inaugurating his domestic service. Seen today in more than 200 countries, CNN International is widely heralded as the prototype for the way in which television will grow into a truly global industry, both as a news and entertainment provider. Turner's larger-than-life personality—combined with the success of CNN domestically—has also elevated him into the American pantheon of entrepreneurs that have been celebrated in this country going back to Morse, Edison, and Ford for technology, and to such early pioneers as Sarnoff and Paley in broadcasting.[1]

But in what sense is CNN International ushering in a new world of global television—distinct from the earlier forms we have described as either international or multinational?

The market for news across borders, like that for television programming (and indeed all economic markets), can be stylized as having both a supply and a demand side. But like most markets, the structure of both sides of the news market is more complicated than the simple binary form suggests. Suppliers and consumers exist at various levels, some primary, some intermediate, and some final. Even these distinctions aren't always firm, since some actors may try to function at more than one level, and technological and regulatory changes may redraw the lines that separate these distinctions, forcing (rather than allowing) actors to compete, both to defend their own markets and enter new ones. Furthermore, markets themselves may overlap in complicated ways that provide a challenge to the clean-minded formalism of economic modeling.

For the moment, it's worth understanding how CNN International functions on the supply side of the market for cross-border news, and how that market itself is changing. (The demand side of the market, and its effects on CNN International and its competitors will be examined in subsequent sections.)

First, a word about the size of the global television trade before looking at its structure. Is there, for example, a fundamental difference between Turner's accomplishment and the earlier two forms we've looked at? In pioneering global news availability, Turner is working in what is perhaps the smallest segment economically of the current cross-border market for television.

Compared to the approximately $5–6 billion currently in international and multinational markets, or the $70–80 billion in domestic programming, the global market—CNN International, its news competitors, plus globally broadcast sports and entertainment such as MTV—together amount to only $400–450 million in revenues. (Entertainment and sports—not news—are far and away the dominant factors in global trade, accounting for well over two-thirds of identifiable revenues.)

Yet Turner is indeed pioneering a new category within the news segment in the television industry. Historically, on an international basis, the economically small market for news trade had heretofore always been confined to two parts: "retail" news sales, and "wholesale" video sales. Before Turner, the final supply of nearly all news—no matter what country it was broadcast in—was exclusively a matter of the domestic news broadcaster gathering it, preparing it, and then distributing it to domestic viewers. In no meaningful sense of the term was news considered international or global, save in the content sense, that every domestic news broadcaster included foreign news along with national and local news as part of the normal news menu.

Today, things are different. News broadcasting—considered in an international sense—can fairly itself be seen as having at least four distinct divisions to it. The first is *global* news broadcasting, exemplified by CNN International, and more recently, by the BBC's World Service Television, both in search of an authentically international mass audience. The second is the related *regional* news broadcasting, of which the newly inaugurated Euronews, Middle East Broadcast

Service, and Televisa's Latin American service are the best-known, each serving a distinct geographical market.

The third market, although decidedly minor economically, is the *retail* market, in which a national television broadcaster sells a domestic news show, or portions of it, to a foreign market. The final category is *wholesale* news, in which generally raw, unedited news footage is sold to multiple broadcasters in many different nations, for final processing, scripting, and delivery as part of a domestic news broadcast.

THE WORRISOME LESSON OF THE RETAILERS

Before looking in detail at what Turner has created with CNN International, and its global and regional competitors, it's worth understanding the retail and wholesale markets, and the forces that have driven them, since many of the same forces are influencing attempts to create a global alternative.

Conceptually, the retail end of the market is an extension into news of the well-established international trade in programming that we've looked at earlier. The news divisions of major broadcast organizations sell their own finished programming, offering foreign markets either a complete program package, or segments that can be incorporated into that nation's regular news programming.

All three American networks, for example, now air their lead evening news shows (as well as some of their so-called reality-based programs) on broadcast systems overseas. *The CBS Evening News* can be seen in more than two dozen countries, as can *60 Minutes* and *48 Hours,* and both ABC and NBC boast a comparable international reach.[2] In recent years—although on an infrequent basis—the same networks have aired segments on their news programs made of material produced originally by foreign broadcasters. A recent episode of *60 Minutes,* for example, carried a segment on Leonid Brezhnev's daughter originally done by Britain's ITN.

This retail supply activity offers some interesting preliminary insights into the demand for news programming that is produced outside a traditional national market. The size of this trade in news is very small in relation to the overall international programming trade.

One study of international television news services finds that retail exports aren't even considered competitively significant by industry observers.[3] Most of it airs on cable or satellite systems that lack the extensive reach of terrestrial over-the-air systems, and generally seems to be viewed heavily by expatriate nationals eager to catch up on home-country coverage. ABC, for example, reported selling $75 million total in entertainment and news programming into overseas markets, barely 2.5 percent of its annual $3 billion revenues.[4] When European viewer studies have looked at national viewing patterns, these foreign retail news shows are barely visible in the surveys—with an actual viewership not unlike those of "community-access" channels in the U.S. cable market.

The problem isn't unique to the American news shows. The BBC transmits its news broadcasts in continental Europe through several cable systems, and claims eight million viewers "able to watch" it; audience survey figures, though, suggest only a tiny fraction of these cable-equipped households actually watch. Overwhelmingly, retail news exports appear to be—economically—virtually inconsequential. Wherever these programs appear (outside their home markets), viewers ignore them in favor of locally produced, local-language news. Executives for American networks, who would speak only off the record, indicate that the news portion of their resale revenues is so small that they are "profitable" only because the production overhead is absorbed as a "sunk cost" by the parent news division.

For those who believe that global news is about to take off, at least in any sense achieving the mass market viewership of domestic television news, this early information from the experience of the retail trade stands as a warning.

WHAT THE WHOLESALERS ARE HAVING TO LEARN

There are additional warnings contained in the experience of the wholesale news operations. This end of the international news business is different from both the retail and global markets. In a real sense, wholesale news isn't an attempt at final supply of global news at all, but rather simply an intermediate supply of foreign news footage, one part in the aggregate system of final supply of news by national broadcasters. Still, because of its lengthy history in gathering and distributing raw news footage around the world, and in dealing with a wide variety of domestic broadcasters, wholesale news offers some intriguing precedents to the would-be final suppliers of global news such as CNN International and BBC/WST.

Since their founding in the 1950s, two London-based agencies, Visnews (since renamed Reuters TV News) and WTN, have dominated the wholesale market for raw news video footage. With each agency holding agreements with several hundred news organizations in seventy-five to one hundred countries, these two agencies function not unlike Reuters, Associated Press, and United Press International, the better-known wire services used by newspapers.

Reuters TV News and WTN—unlike the wire services—don't provide finished copy, but rather supply barely distilled news footage, which individual television news departments edit, script, and incorporate into their broadcasts. The obvious advantage for broadcasters is in cost savings—opening an average overseas bureau can cost $250,000 or more per year, and 99 percent of footage shot is never broadcast.[5]

With the number of channels and total broadcasting hours—including news broadcasting—rising enormously, one might think that wholesalers would be enjoying salad days and record profits. But there are a host of signs that wholesalers—even though they hold a larger market share of the international news business than the retailers—are not doing well.

The thirty-six-year-old Visnews, the largest of the wholesalers, became a wholly owned division of Reuters, when the latter bought out its partners in 1992. Claiming the purchase price was too small to be "material to shareholders," the $3 billion Reuters noted that the wholesale agency had been contributing barely $113 million to the parent company in revenues. Reuters said it planned to undertake a "large cash investment" in the wholesaler, after recent declines in its revenues, and only modest profits, and intended to integrate the units's news-gathering personnel into Reuters' larger network of print, radio, and television correspondents.[6]

At the smaller WTN (80 percent owned by Cap Cities/ABC), the growth of potential new outlets likewise hasn't apparently brought a commensurate surge in sales or profits. With 1990 revenues of $35.5 million, WTN earned a slim $1.3 million in profits, after barely making money in the late 1980s. Although ABC doesn't provide separate 1991 or 1992 figures for WTN, a recent *New York Times* article reported that both WTN and Reuters TV News were "often barely profitable,"[7] and that the two agencies had held merger talks in 1991. The talks failed, in part because competing channels wanted exclusive rights to one or the other agency's video, and the two agencies feared consolidation would slash the size of the remaining one organization.

HOW THE TELEVISION NEWS BUSINESS IS CHANGING WORLDWIDE

One important reason why the wholesalers aren't looking robust these days has to do with the restructuring of news-gathering that is hitting the television industry worldwide.

In the United States, when Ted Turner launched his domestic CNN system in 1980, he faced networks that were spending $100–150 million a year on their news divisions. Turner was budgeting $25–30 million to offer twenty-four-hour-a-day service. To survive, as one analyst put it, "the existing financial structure of the networks would have to be turned upside down."[8]

Turner's strategy followed three simple rules: computerize, economize, and piggyback. From the start, Turner took advantage of the latest in computer and satellite technology that would allow the company to integrate newswires, the assignment desk, producers, graphics rundowns, tape lists, and anchor scripts. CNN thus became the creator of television's first truly "electronic newsroom."

To economize, they coupled that with a hiring policy that was long on new talent—often just out of college—at the wages CNN wanted to pay. The company then added a few more seasoned journalists such as Daniel Schorr, Bernard Shaw, and George Watson willing to work at substantially below network scale.

Turner's innovation proved its worth almost immediately—nowhere more clearly than in the cost-savings reaped by hiring junior staff for long hours with no fixed work rules and low pay. Christened "video journalists" (VJs) a bit grandly by CNN, "the so-called VJs wrote, produced, edited tape, ran cameras, and operated control-room equipment"—often several different things in one long day.

Network journalists grumbled about the sometime amateurish consequences—lost picture feeds, wrong open mikes, flubbed graphics, but as one critic put it, "in this one massive stroke, CNN destroyed fifty accumulated years of network work rules. VJs were paid just above minimum wage, apprentices to a system they were helping to invent as they went along."[9]

Faced already with local UHF stations, and now a burgeoning cable market that began to bleed away viewers and ad revenues, the networks retaliated with their own cost-cutting and technological innovation. Starting in the mid-1980s, CBS, NBC, and ABC all began extensive layoffs, numbering in the hundreds and covering everyone from journalists earning six figures to office assistants and secretaries. ABC alone in the 1980s shed 300 of its 1,450 news employees.

Piggybacking proved its worth almost immediately on the international front, as CNN turned to foreign broadcasters to provide video footage of international events. The networks had traditionally disdained such sources, relying instead on their own overseas bureaus and the wholesale agencies. By using other broadcasters' footage, Turner could avoid the high costs of network-style foreign bureaus and yet still get the story. In effect, he was pioneering a "co-op" strategy of shared news among broadcasters, since in exchange for this foreign footage, CNN made its own domestic footage available to overseas partners.

In Europe, a similar revolution got underway as the number of private channels exploded. There too the drive to computerize, economize, and piggyback drove both the new private broadcasters who were seeking audience at the lowest feasible cost and the big public broadcasters who found their heavily staffed organizations under greater and greater pressure to compete. Extensive computerization of newsrooms was implemented, news staffs were pruned back, and more and more broadcasters turned to others to provide footage that went into covering international stories.

Among the wholesalers, Reuters TV and WTN haven't escaped these same pressures. Revenue growth from its core activity—news-gathering—has been the chief disappointment. Like the programming trade, both service and selling price in the wholesale business sharply decline as the customer base moves from a handful of broadcasters in the industrial West to the government monopolies that still dominate the Third World. According to Phil Lines, Reuters TV's group marketing manager, annual subscriptions range from several million dollars (for a large Western network that receives daily satellite feeds of all the agency's footage and access to its library), to the low tens of thousands (for Third World stations that get one videocassette a week, shipped airmail).

Because of restructuring, ironically, it's been at the wealthy traditional top end of the price chain—in the United States and Europe, where channel choice and broadcast time have proliferated most rapidly—that the wholesalers find themselves faced with eroding revenues. CBS, after several years with WTN, switched to Reuters TV recently, at a price reportedly much less than the $1 million a year it had been paying WTN. Meanwhile, Reuters TV was significantly damaged when Rupert Murdoch's Sky News, after initially signing a five-year, $50 million contract, cited mounting losses of its own and forced renegotiation of its contract at heavily reduced rates.

In response, Reuters TV and WTN have set out to cut their own costs—and generate alternative revenues. Reuters TV currently staffs thirty-five bureaus around the world, compared to Reuters' 118 (WTN has fifteen). Reuters' announced plans are to consolidate many of these bureaus, and to continue trimming its subsidiary's 440-member staff. Additionally, it intends to make much greater use of freelance "contract" crews on an ad hoc basis, hoping local nationals (paid local wages) will significantly reduce basic news-gathering costs.

None of the problems facing the wholesale agencies suggest they will disappear any time soon. To the contrary, with broadcasters everywhere reluctant to set up expensive foreign bureaus, wholesalers will continue to maintain their customer base. The challenge is not for customers, but for revenues and profits.

Broadcasting via satellite doesn't by itself give an upper hand to an enterprise like CNN International over national broadcasters. As the technology is diffused, those national broadcasters are able to tap into global satellite news sources on their own, through agencies such as Reuters or WTN, or through co-op relations with broadcasters in other countries. As a result, the gathering of foreign news stories remains a national (or even local) activity, directed at national (or local) audiences, and satellites serve as a transmission technology, rather than the foundation for a set of truly global broadcasters whose common audience would span the planet.

In such a world, as we shall see in the next chapter, in the competition for mass audiences across borders, national news programs retain distinct advantages over the globals: the ability to follow a recognized format at a recognized time of day and to use anchors and reporters who speak the same language as the viewer, with a subtle grasp of national tastes, biases, and viewpoints. The success of the globals rests less on their ability to supply global-style news than on their ability to identify the audiences and advertisers that are demanding it.

6

MASS MEDIUM OR OFFICE INTERCOM — WILL THE GLOBALS' EXPERIENCE BE DIFFERENT?

G iven a microscopic retail news trade and a wholesale news industry totalling under $200 million after forty years, and with broadcasters constantly searching for cost-cutting alternatives, an obvious question arises. Will the new global networks (and their regional cousins) be able to overcome the minor economic role, and fragile profit performance, of both the wholesalers and retailers?

CNN certainly thinks so. Ted Turner has repeatedly insisted that his vision for a world television news network was always driven first by idealism—"the salvation of life on earth," as he once put it—rather than making money. (More specifically, as he told *Time* several years ago, "I want to start dealing with issues like disarmament, pollution, soil erosion, population control, alternative energy sources.")[1]

In official statements, CNN's President Tom Johnson echoes his chief's ideas:

> Our vision is global. During the next five years, our highest priority will be given to the expansion of the CNN International network itself. Beyond that, we look to establish some new strategic alliances which may enable us to serve in the language of the regions such as Germany, Japan, and Russia. Our aspiration is to be able to report from virtually any point on the globe, to every point on the globe.[2]

But how exactly does Turner's heroic vision get translated into the competitive economics of the broadcast business? More concretely,

having examined the problems facing the supply side of markets for
international news, is there a way to see the demand side offering a
clearer future for global news?

Robert Ross, as head of TBS International, is the man charged
with making Turner's vision a business reality. As he explains, the
demand side is more than just a simple matter of competing global
networks:

> There may be room for one or two, even three, global English-
> language networks. But clearly there's room for some region-
> al ones. There's going to be a Spanish-language network in
> South America, there's going to be a news network in Japan
> in Japanese, there's probably going to be a French one which
> will go into French West Africa, and there will probably be
> an Arabic one. And our long-term thinking is to try to take a
> 30 to 40 percent interest in each of these, help them set it up
> and operate it, and at the same time to make each one a news
> supplier to the others, thus lowering news-gathering costs.[3]

The growth of CNN International's reach since its founding is
constantly being remarked upon (while Ross's description—of a very
different global vision—is simultaneously ignored or glossed over, a
matter we shall turn to). From a small base its first several years, the
number of countries receiving the service had reached eighty by 1990,
and by late 1993, the number was over 200—virtual global saturation.

But as critics and competitors are quick to point out, CNN International's "reach" is substantially broader than it is deep. Although
more than five billion people in theory can now see CNN
International, the actual number of viewers capable of receiving
Turner's news programming (according to CNN International's own
estimates) amounts to less than 73 million households—slightly more,
that is, across the entire world outside the United States than the 63
million households who can view CNN inside the United States.[4] In
many of the countries serviced by CNN International, in fact, apart
from a handful of elite households and government offices, luxury
hotels catering to Western business travelers and tourists are the core
of these local audiences.

Put slightly differently, in the United States, CNN reaches an
impressive 60 percent of U.S. television households. Outside the
United States, however, CNN International's own estimate of its audience as a percent of the world's population amounts to slightly more
than 1 percent. Even this 1 percent figure, however, overstates the

global broadcaster's actual viewers around the world. There is an easily missed subtlety when CNN talks about its 73 million audience or reach, not always understood by a layperson. *Audience*, as used here doesn't refer to a group of television viewers actually watching a given program at any given moment, or even a group who watches a channel over any set period of time. Rather, it refers to the number of people who, if they turned on their television sets and tuned to the channel, could watch it. This use of the term is hardly unique to CNN—actually, it is standard in most discussion of cable or satellite viewing; but it is significantly different from, say, a Nielsen rating of an audience for an American television program.

Put another way, the American public network PBS could fairly claim—if talking about its audience or reach as CNN International does—to have a U.S. audience approaching 90 million households, since most American households are capable of receiving their local PBS affiliate. No one, of course, gives the slightest attention to such figures, since on any given evening PBS is quite happy when it draws three or four million actual viewers for its programming.

As it turns out, the number of people watching CNN International globally at any time amounts at most to a few hundred thousand, perhaps half a million—not the 73 million spoken of so casually as CNN International's audience. (By comparison, in the United States, where CNN's audience is monitored, average viewership is 400,000 out of its 63 million potential viewers.)[5]

Even the issue itself of the larger-sounding international audience—CNN International's 73 million, for example—is open to dispute. The standard television audience rating services, such as Nielsen, cover very few countries. Consequently, the numbers used by global broadcasters tend to be a combination of fact, guess, and hopes. Peter Vesey, CNN International's vice president, readily acknowledges, for example, that only about 40 million of the 73 million CNN International claims are "legal and paid" viewing numbers. That is, only 40 million come from rated cable and satellite viewing services in Western Europe, plus a handful elsewhere. The rest are the company's best-guess extrapolations.[6]

This discrepancy between the quite large-sounding audience or reach and actual viewership of global broadcasters has led to a host of cautionary warnings from some television industry professionals about the progress of the industry generally. Rich Zahradnik, editor of the trade journal *Television Business International*, for example, now distinguishes between what he calls CNN International's "influence" and "business." Zahradnik credits CNN International with an initial success in achieving global influence and recognition, while insisting that the jury is still out on its future as a lucrative business. In a memorably apt summary of the situation, Zahradnik says he wonders whether CNN International isn't headed toward winning a global mass-market viewership so much as it is destined to be "the office intercom of the global elites."[7]

The discrepancy between audience and actual viewership, though, isn't the only reason why Zahradnik and other professionals are skeptical about CNN International's global growth horizon. The barriers CNN International faces are not unlike those facing other would-be global or major regional satellite services, whether for news exclusively or for a full range of news, entertainment, movie, and sports programming.

The issue—as CNN International's ability to transmit a signal that blankets the globe demonstrates—is not of *technologically feasible supply*, but fundamentally of *economically viable demand*. Having proved that television signals can be sent around the physical world, the questions are the real-world socioeconomic gatekeeping issues that have faced commercial television broadcasting since the beginning: Who will watch, who will pay (and how much), and why?

Whether one looks at CNN International, BBC/WST, Star TV, MBC, BSkyB, or a proliferating number of other would-be satellite-based transnational broadcasters, these issues remain the same. Concentrating on CNN International, to begin with, can quickly bring those issues into focus and suggests why both the popular vision of CNN International as a global mass medium and the much different sketch of what Robert Ross sees as a viable business opportunity based on corporate multinational investment remain to be decided.

HOW CNN INTERNATIONAL HOPES TO MAKE MONEY

CNN's management doesn't formally report CNN International's total income and profitability, but executives have at times orally indicated general performance levels. In 1991, Peter Vesey, for example, claimed that CNN International expected to gross $28 million and was "nearly breakeven." Faced soon afterward with the launch of BBC/WTV more recently, Vesey would say only of profit performance that CNN International was "covering its bills," and that he expected the parent company to double its investment. By 1994, Vesey claimed that gross income had soared to "about $100 million," but would offer no comment on profitability. With Turner Broadcasting grossing over $1.14

billion, and its CNN division domestically reporting revenues approaching $500 million alone, even $100 million is a relatively modest business for Ted Turner. Similarly, with BBC/WST, Sky News, MBC, and others all reporting similarly modest numbers, the obvious question is whether it will remain so.

To answer the question requires examining the multiple sources of presumed future revenues, and their likelihood for growth, in order to assess the economic potential underlying CNN International's (or BBC/WST's or the regional satellite broadcasters') future. At present, apart from parent company support, CNN International's revenues derive essentially from four principal sources: hotel fees, rebroadcast fees, direct viewer fees, and advertising.

Hotel fees obviously start from a small audience and income base, compared to the world's television audience. CNN International, for example, relies on 1300 hotels in Europe as its core market, while BBC/WST reports being in fewer than 350 hotels globally.[8] Hotel viewer fees also face a slow growth horizon, because such fees are paid almost exclusively by international chains and luxury hotels catering to an English-speaking market of business travelers and tourists. Given the small number of such luxury hotels (and extensive piracy of CNN International's signal by many hotels), full saturation of such a market—especially outside the industrial world—leaves any global broadcaster with revenues in the low millions of dollars at best.

Rebroadcast or "carriage" fees are paid by a local broadcaster or cable company for the right to carry CNN International or BBC/WST as part of its regular programming. But these likewise face a relatively low slope in revenue growth. The low fees paid by most countries for programming in international trade—amounting often to a few thousand dollars per program (as shown in Table 2.2)—leave CNN International able to command—even in larger, affluent markets—decidedly less revenue than the parent CNN earns from its U.S. market.

In Western Europe, for example, CNN International claims it reaches 23 million cable homes plus another 14 million via Astra satellite—60 percent of its global audience currently. Yet CNN International faces several difficult challenges: first, the existence of well-developed and highly watched over-the-air local news broadcasters, both public and private; second, the still-low penetration levels of both cable and satellite; and third—in countries such as Germany—the problem of "reverse carriage" fees, in which CNN or other program services must pay, rather than being paid, for appearing on the country's cable system. In short, the quest for an economically profitable audience even in affluent Europe remains a daunting one.

HOW BIG ARE THE HOME SATELLITE AND CABLE MARKETS GLOBALLY?

The potential for upward growth of such fees, of course, depends a great deal on the audience share CNN International is able to capture in competition with domestic alternatives, particularly domestic news programming. Here again, the global network faces a decidedly large challenge.

In the mid-1980s, when CNN International was launched, the conventional wisdom was that satellite and cable technology was about to transform the global market for television viewing, increasing immensely both total global viewing and the number of channels available. The prevalent view was that these new technologies would erode rather quickly the nationally based, over-the-air systems that preceded them.

But a decade later, the advance of cable and satellite systems and their ability to displace existing national broadcasters seems less decisive. Outside the United States (where cable and satellite together reach two-thirds of homes), neither cable nor satellite-to-home broadcasting has achieved similar gains. In Western Europe (collectively, the world's second richest television market), both home satellite and cable lag well behind U.S. penetration rates.

The issue isn't one of supply. Well over one hundred separate European channels are broadcast by satellite, for example, yet one recent report places home satellite reception at approximately six million households, or 5.4 percent of total television households, with Germany and the United Kingdom comprising over two-thirds of the total.[9]

European cable has done better, reaching an estimated thirty million homes, or 26 percent of regional households. But these figures too are heavily weighted by Germany and the United Kingdom. With minor exceptions (the Benelux countries and Switzerland), much of Europe remains virtually untouched by cable. France, for example, has a combined satellite/cable penetration rate of 6 percent of households, Spain 9 percent, Italy less than 1 percent; even the United Kingdom, with the second largest number of satellite and cable connections after Germany, has barely an 18 percent penetration of its television households. Research suggests that European acceptance of cable and satellite won't approach U.S. levels until after the turn of the century.[10]

In Japan, the world's third largest market (and home to vibrant television and electronics industries), the European experience holds true. With more than forty-one million television households, fewer than 15 percent have elected either satellite or cable options, although both are widely available.

Throughout the rest of the world, cable and satellite-to-home broadcasting are spreading even more slowly. In Latin America, for example, satellite and cable usage is best described as "fledgling." Brazil reports 1 percent satellite penetration of its thirty million television households (out of 150 million population), and a cable percentage probably under 6 percent (signal pirating is extensive). Mexico, the region's second largest country, has less than 10 percent combined penetration. Colombia reports under 9 percent combined; Venezuela, under 5 percent. From there, the percentage penetration by satellite and cable drops in other countries to less than 2 percent.

The penetration of satellite and cable into the Middle East and Africa don't even reach Latin American levels. The Middle East Broadcast Center, which broadcasts a pan-Arab-World signal via satellite from London, estimates perhaps 400,000 home-receiving dishes throughout the region. In Africa, reception of South Africa's M-Net signal, which blankets the continent, is picked up by an inconsequentially small number of dishes. "Apart from white farmers and government officials," says *Television Business International* editor Rich Zahradnik, "it's hard to tell who's watching."[11]

More recently, the Asian market has been seen as a potential gold mine for home satellite reception. Two recent *New York Times* stories illustrate what seems to be the vast opportunities awaiting satellite transmission among the 2.6 billion residents of Asia.

One article, about India, tells the story of the "dish-wallahs," individual entrepreneurs who install a satellite dish atop an urban apartment building, then run cabling to individual apartments and sell the programming received for a monthly fee.[12] The story is almost a model for how the promise of "global television" is often described, with talks of the "thousands of apartment buildings, and millions of their inhabitants in major Indian cities" that receiving everything from CNN International to MTV. But, in fact, when the story offers actual numbers—in a country of 880 million—the best estimates turn out to be 3.3 million households able to receive such global television (compared to 40 million households for Indian state broadcaster, Doordarshan). Moreover, among these 3.3 million households, BBC/WST's regular actual viewership, for example, averaged little more than 100,000.

More recently, the *Times* has discovered a similar phenomenon in China. In a front-page story, "Satellites Bring Information Revolution to China," the newspaper celebrates "the hundreds of thousands of satellite dishes that are sprouting, as the Chinese say, like bamboo shoots after a spring rain."[13] It goes on to emphasize the government's consequent loss of control over television viewing and the extensive popularity of satellite television viewing among the Chinese masses. But as in India, the actual numbers of such viewers—4.8 million households, among more than one billion Chinese—tend on modest reflection to deflate the imminent character of the satellite-based "revolution" captured in the story's headline, especially since the dish alone sells for more than the average Chinese's $360 per capita income.

What's obviously noteworthy about both stories is how deeply they draw on the initial confidence posed for satellite home delivery, not only as an enormous business opportunity, but as a means of increasing press and personal freedom in countries whose governments limit both. To journalists and democrats alike, indeed, the political "leap-frogging" ability of satellite home delivery—what some have likened to the role of short wave radio during World War II and later the cold war—made its dispersion deeply attractive, whatever the business opportunities.

But in seeking to establish market beachheads around the world, the global systems have proved themselves to be less than fully interested in "leap-frogging" local governments, in order to provide direct access to information by citizens. CNN International allows the local broadcaster (often a government monopoly) that carries it to edit or alter CNN International material as it might wish before any local rebroadcast.

Thus, for example, when CNN International signed an agreement with the Indonesian government for carriage by Indonesia's Palapa satellite (which reaches much of Southeast Asia), CNN willingly agreed to allow the Indonesian government to edit its signal. Peter Vesey readily acknowledged the reason. "We want to do the right thing," he was quoted in a Reuters interview, "by working with the authorities and respecting the cultural and political concerns that might keep us out of the region."[14]

Vesey today insists that he was misquoted—but then does acknowledge that where CNN International is picked up and then rebroadcast locally, either by cable or over-the-air, "we give broad free access to our signal, and the locals are free to edit or excerpt it, as long as they carry it as their own. Of course, they can shut us off."[15]

A starker example of global broadcasters' vulnerability to government power came months after Star TV was purchased by Rupert Murdoch. Aware that the Chinese government had been angered by BBC/WST broadcasts on several occasions, and that the government had announced a ban on satellite dishes to regain control over its airwaves, Murdoch peremptorily dropped the BBC from Star entirely.

Apart from whether the new era of global television will bring new information rights to billions of people, there is still the question of how many will be watching global television—at least via satellite and cable—over the rest of this century. A study by the private, for-profit CIT Research suggests that direct-to-home satellite penetration of the Asia-Pacific region will in fact grow, but only from a current base of 1.8 percent of television-equipped homes to an estimated 6.2 percent by 2002.[16] The compelling point is that, far from being a means of mass communications, in the sense at least one associates with television, satellite-to-home television is likely to remain a decidedly up-market enterprise, focused heavily on the Third World's emerging but tiny middle and upper-middle classes.

WHO WILL PAY FOR SATELLITE AND CABLE TELEVISION?

For the would-be global network, such low penetration figures highlight two other difficulties. The first is associated with viewer-based revenues. By the late 1970s, as early satellite programming took off in the United States, programmers found that freelance "pirating" of their signal by home-satellite viewers threatened potential revenues; to solve the problem, they began to encrypt their signals, limiting viewership to those who paid for a "descrambler" attached to the home dish.

In Europe, more and more satellite-based programming follows the same pattern.[17] In England, for example, to view most programming carried by the Astra satellite (including Sky News, Britain's regional competitor with CNN International) requires "smart cards" to descramble the satellite signal. Unlike earlier efforts to block piracy, these "smart cards" are increasingly sophisticated, and potentially remotely programmable, thus making "free" satellite television almost as impossible as the once-debated issue of "free" software so beloved by the more anarchically inclined among computer hackers.

The conflicting desire of satellite-based television—on the one hand, to maximize audience, and at the same time to be paid for the audience it reaches—shows up in the indecision of BBC/WST about how it will eventually be paid for the programming it provides. WST is a Thatcher-era-born attempt to bring the BBC into the world of commercial, profit-driven broadcasting. It receives no direct funding from the parent corporation or the British government, and so has been launched in Asia in partnership with Star TV, a Hong Kong-based broadcaster that agreed to share part of its satellite ad revenues with WST.

BBC and Star TV made the decision to use an unscrambled signal, available therefore without charge to anyone with a dish and willingness to view it. The market rationale was the need to gain early audience, and thereby build a case for advertising that would replace foregone viewer fees.

By 1993, WST claimed to be pleased with its initial penetration of the Asian market—11 million households, according to research commissioned by Star TV, were able to receive the programming. The service appeared to be especially strong in India, where WST president Chris Irwin said they had quickly outpaced CNN International in popularity, and were reaching some 3.3 million households.

But Irwin was also acutely aware of the challenge facing a global broadcaster such as the English-only BBC/WST. Doordarshan, the Indian government broadcasting monopoly (with more than 40 million viewer households and over $120 million in ad revenues) had already announced plans to set up three Hindi-language satellite channels of its own—offering news, sports, and entertainment. Meanwhile, a new private satellite television service, called Zee TV, had begun broadcasting an exclusively Hindi-language channel. "We have audiences everywhere," said Subhash Chandra, Zee TV's chairman. "[Unlike BBC/WST, we can reach] the villages where people don't speak English," a condition that accurately describes 90 percent of India's potential television audience.[18]

This willingness on the part of both public and private national broadcasters to confront the globals with vernacular, nationally based alternatives goes to the heart of the problem the globals are facing in building audience. Having utilized the rapidly falling price of satellite communications to construct international networks, they are seeing challengers emerge, using the same technology, but with a much narrower single-country (or single-language) focus, albeit often with the potential to reach huge markets, such as India and China.

Irwin, coming from the BBC's environment of public service broadcasting, insisted that he welcomed the challenges, and saw them benefiting all parties. "One thing is clear," he said, "the days of state broadcasting monopolies are gone." But he then went on to observe,

> That is not to say that the days of national broadcasting are over even if monopoly is no more. Neither the BBC nor any other international broadcaster can replace the indigenous broadcaster. . . . The instinct for self-preservation is as strong amongst broadcasters as amongst anyone. BBC World Service Television may have beaten Doordarshan by five days with pictures of last October's earthquake in the Uttar Karshi district. My guess is that next time Doordarshan won't be

quite so slow off the mark, on this or on other stories of consequence for India. Its credibility ultimately depends on it being able to cover the news on its doorstep.[19]

Irwin's point about Doordarshan can be multiplied throughout much of Asia. National satellite systems are taking off in the region's midsized countries: Thailand is scheduled to launch a satellite that will broadcast exclusively in Thai, and both Korea and Malaysia will have their own vernacular systems aloft soon thereafter. China, meanwhile, has two satellites of its own on order, and Indonesia is set to launch its third generation Palapa-C1 in 1995. All told in Asia, nearly a dozen national and regional satellites are set for launch in the next two years, with more to follow.

The proliferation of these satellite alternatives, especially those targeted in local languages, cuts to the very heart of the growth strategy foreseen by the globals. That strategy was actually never meant to turn satellite-based viewing into a mass medium as we casually understand television, but instead to "skim the cream" off the growing (but still relatively small) upper-middle-class television-watching portion of the vast Asian audience. Current figures indicate that, among Star TV's viewer footprint of 2.6 billion, 25 million households have incomes above $30,000 a year, a number expected to double by the year 2000.

Star TV, like other satellite-based services, although launched as a free-to-view system, gradually foresees conversion to a pay-television subscription format for much if not all of its programming.[20] Free viewing has been meant as an audience-building prelude among the Asian middle classes, who would then be persuaded—with, in theory, limited over-the-air alternatives domestically—that paying for the privilege to receive CNN or BBC or movies or sports was worth the price.

Hugh Williams, Irwin's deputy at BBC/WST and head of programming, is quite frank about the limits such ambitions place on the future for the would-be global news broadcasters. "We accept the fact that we will in some sense always be a secondary service," he says in regard to competing with local news broadcasters. Even in Asia, where the BBC/WST was proud of the eleven million households it was reaching, he acknowledged that actual active viewership at any time was closer to 2 to 3 percent of those households (that is, 200,000 to 300,000 people in Asia), and that "viewer subscription, not advertising, will be the big piece of our future revenue."[21]

But the emergence of satellite-driven national systems is reshaping that future. Rather than building on the technological uniqueness of being satellite-based and thus available eventually to the top 5 to 10 percent of the Asian market, Star TV—even before its purchase by Rupert Murdoch—realized that it needed to compete in the more mundane (and nontechnological) world of programming mix and audience tastes that has always faced competitive national broadcasters, whatever the means of delivery. And faced with widely divergent tastes, customs, and preferences among the thirty-eight countries now receiving Star TV's signal, the question is—even with Murdoch—whether the company can succeed.

Julian Mounter, Star TV's CEO before Murdoch took over, was already trying to recast the company's operating strategy by describing its structural evolution into the form of what he called a "jellyfish"—with separate movie, news, business, entertainment, and children's channels, each in turn translated, in tentacle-like fashion, into six of the region's main language groups. But he acknowledged the very real problem he faced, even if such a strategy—presenting a thick web of technical, financial, and consumer acceptance problems—could be implemented. "The question is how long a lead time we have until the broadcasters in the 38 countries wake up to the competition from us," Mounter admitted. "We have to continue driving our reach to such a size to provide ourselves with the financing to buy better programming."[22]

In July, 1993, the fate of Star TV took a sudden new turn with announcement that Rupert Murdoch's News Corporation had paid $525 million in stock and cash for 64 percent of the Asian satellite broadcaster. Entry of Murdoch into the Asian television market alone might indicate a brightly ambitious future, but as the British journal the *Economist* noted: "In buying into Star TV, Mr. Murdoch is buying into the idea of a middle-class Asia. It is a speculative buy . . . a Murdoch-powered Star network is going to face immense difficulties in making money throughout Asia."[23] One can reasonably ask, apart from Murdoch's optimism about the market, why—so soon after launch—a deep-pocketed Li, much more intimately acquainted with the region, was ready to bow out.

IF NOT VIEWERS, WILL ADVERTISERS PAY FOR GLOBAL TELEVISION?

Whoever owns Star TV leaves open the crucial question of where its revenues—and profits—will come from in the years ahead. Julian Mounter's solution—building maximum audience first—meant that although Star TV was planning to start up three new subscription channels, it would continue staying focused on its free-to-air, advertising-based strategy; to date, Murdoch also seems to be delaying introduction of pay television while Star TV builds audience.

But making advertising work on a global system is the second of the two great revenue questions facing viability of the medium. Faced with multilingual, multinational audiences, the challenge that the satellite-based broadcaster must meet is not merely of audience size, but efficient reach.

Even though Star TV now claims to have nearly quadrupled its early viewing audience of eleven million households, like CNN International and other would-be global or large regional operators, it faces the complex task of convincing sophisticated advertisers that its enormous audience reach over time offers a preferred alternative to nationally or vernacular-based broadcast alternatives, whether delivered by satellite, cable, or over-the-air terrestrial means.

Star TV itself seems inordinately aware of the problem. In order to win initial advertiser interest in a pan-Asian service, under Li Ka-shing's ownership, it reportedly offered not only rock-bottom prices (as little as $500 for a thirty-second spot), but even sweetened some deal with warrants for eventual purchase of shares in HutchVision, Star TV's corporate parent. Now under Murdoch, the private company does not release detailed financial statements, but claims to be making substantial headway in ad sales. Industry sources believe Star TV's five channels may have grossed close to $100 million in 1992, and should have done at least as well in 1993.

But with $500 million already invested in the company, and the need to substantially share revenues with the programmers for their costs, as well as to upgrade programming, the chances for large-scale financial success are far from certain—no doubt the reason why Li was so willing to transfer his risk to Murdoch. Yet even with the programming opportunities Murdoch brings (through control of Fox Studios, and its library), he must face the revenue issue head-on. As the *Economist* underscored in its article on the Murdoch takeover, subscription and cable fees (plus local, not global, advertising) are key. Relationships with local cable operators, and even more so, with local regulators, will play as large a part in Star TV's future as Murdoch's money or programming savvy.

Ultimately, with time and additional investment, Star TV certainly could become profitable. But in doing so, it is far from likely to become what has been held out as the potential for global television—a mass medium, reaching out through its vast footprint to Asia's billions of inhabitants, as historically free, over-the-air terrestrial broadcasting did in the industrial West from the 1950s on.

WHEN THE ADVERTISERS SPEAK, WHO LISTENS—AND HOW?

The dilemma Star TV faces in attempting to find a large and lucrative market position—as distinct from a technologically feasible one—is by no means unique to the vast, but relatively undeveloped economies of Asia.

In Europe over the last decade, attempts to establish both pan-European broadcasting and advertising have met numerous problems. During the early 1980s, when Saatchi & Saatchi and a few other giant ad agencies were driving international consolidation of the industry, there was brisk and expansive talk about the imminence of global advertising that would form the revenue base for global broadcasting. Coca-Cola, Sony, and other consumer producers with a strong brand-name recognition were thought to be models for a revolution in consumer advertising that would profoundly reshape the entire advertising market.

A decade later, the promise of such a "global ad market" is decidedly dimmer than its advocates had hoped. As a Coca-Cola executive recently commented, "We're not in the business of looking for a global, or even regional, strategy per se any more. We're concentrating on national, or sometimes common-language markets such as Germany and Austria. For us, globalism is still off in the future."[24] Columbia University media critic Les Brown makes much the same point:

> There really are very few brands—Coke, Pepsi, Sony, Panasonic, IBM—maybe 20 or so, total, that are truly global in terms of recognition. And individual markets can vary enormously, with only a slight difference in packaging or presentation meaning the difference between success and failure. When you watch CNN overseas, as I have, you're constantly struck by how little real advertising they carry.[25]

Global network executives themselves readily acknowledge the problems they are having in attracting substantial advertising, especially of the vaunted multinational kind. Peter Vesey, for example, notes that "regional advertising is still a new category for us, and we're having to work hard to create it." (Advertising overall accounts for about 35 to 40 percent of CNN International's income, according to Vesey.)[26]

The heart of the limits faced by both advertisers and programmers in Europe is linguistic, and relates to the question of economic efficiency for advertisers. Satellites can deliver programming and advertising instantaneously and simultaneously across the more than two dozen languages spoken in Western Europe, but the viewers—as repeated market research shows—want their television delivered in local tongues. Contrary to a history in which both motion pictures and early television broadcasts relied heavily on dubbing of foreign (often U.S.) programming, an affluent and culturally confident Europe now appears to be more linguistically divided than ever before.

One study, for example, entitled "The Last Frontiers of European Television," concluded:

> While national boundaries have been eroded by technology, and deregulation and privatization have generated more and more channels, pan-European broadcasting projects have failed to hit the mark. . . . [B]roadcasters have stopped thinking in ambitious pan-European terms and begun concentration on language markets. Of the ten advertising-supported satellite-delivered TV channels with pan-European ambitions currently in operation, none is remotely near the break-even point.[27]

Other research has turned up additional information discomfiting to would-be global or super-regional broadcasters (such as CNN International or BBC/WST). They've heavily staked their growth plans on English-language broadcasting, on the assumption that English is Europe's (if not the globe's) new *lingua franca*. Using English, they had reasoned, could at least in part surmount the language divisions of Europe—and target affluent, English-speaking viewers on the Continent.

But when ad researchers recently tested 4,500 Europeans for "perceived" versus "actual" English-language skills, the results were discouraging. First, the interviewees were asked to evaluate their English-language abilities, and then to translate a series of sample English phrases or sentences. The study produced, in its own words, "sobering" results: "the number of people really fit for English-language television turned out to be less than half the expected audience." In countries such as France, Spain, and Italy, the study found, fewer than 3 percent had excellent command of English; only in small markets, such as Scandinavia and the Low Countries did the numbers even exceed 10 percent.[28]

These barriers to common programming and advertising run contrary to the widespread impression—held by many American and European cultural figures—that the opening up of European television in the 1980s would in turn open floodgates through which would pour a vast river of American programming. A core assumption of many versions of globalization has been that English particularly—taught today in so many countries—would produce an increasingly homogeneous audience for programming.

In fact, the sharp increase in the number of European channels (from about thirty in the early 1970s to almost 150 today) has significantly increased domestically produced European programming. One study, in late 1989, looking askance at the protracted battle Europeans had fought over whether to limit program imports (finally set forth in the European Union's "Television Without Frontiers" directive) concluded, "One can't help but wonder what all the fuss [was] about." Using carefully weighted ratings that measured not only hours of programming but audience penetration, the study—based on seventy channels in eighteen countries—found that the average European content in European television was 68 percent. A European Broadcast Union (EBU) study published three years later (but using slightly different coefficients) found that 85 percent of European programming was not merely European, but limited to its country of origin (thus excluding intra-European imports).[29]

Given what we already know about the relatively low cost of importing American programming (from Table 2.2), this should come as a surprise. After all, wouldn't presumably rational economic actors (that is, the European broadcasters) prefer to continue buying cheap American programming, as they have for almost forty years, rather than engage in expensive domestic production? Ironically, that assumption misunderstands the effect of competition that the growth of private channels and the commercialization of public channels introduced into the European marketplace, an effect that is spreading and will continue to spread into global markets as competition among nationally based broadcasters (to say nothing of satellite-based systems) grow larger.

What we now can see clearly is that the historic group of monopsonies (that is, the monopoly of buyers, not sellers) represented by the old public broadcast systems held down the price paid for imported programming. With no competitors, they could substantially dictate to program producers the price they would pay—and since most of the American programming constituted reruns of shows, whose costs had already been (theoretically) recovered in the U.S. market, the program producers went along with the situation.

As increasing numbers of channels developed a ravenous appetite for programming to fill out their broadcast schedules in the 1980s, American producers had a vision of unlimited, ever-expanding revenues—while European cultural elites saw the specter of a grotesque

Americanization of European values and beliefs. What neither counted on was that the competitive bidding-up of prices paid for American programming stimulated European broadcasters to begin looking for alternatives to an ever-rising input horizon. Domestic programming, which once seemed so costly compared to American reruns, now suddenly was only somewhat more expensive—and the dispersed risk accompanying coproduction could remove even that cost differential.

The additional fact was that, given a choice, European audiences preferred domestic programming to American imports. Back in the days when public monopoly broadcasters had limited viewing choices to one or two stations, the low cost of imports had been a magnetic attraction to the broadcasters. In turn, it had spawned the idea (among Americans especially) that American television was not only immensely popular with Europeans, but that Europeans were uniquely willing (compared to Americans) to accept dubbing or subtitling with their viewing fare. With competition, low costs were replaced by optimizing profits—profits that could be won by delivering the largest audiences to advertisers willing to pay for those audiences. And that in turn has produced an entirely new perception of what Europeans actually prefer to watch.

By late 1993, a comprehensive survey of prime-time viewing around the world underscored just how significant the role of domestic, as distinct from international, programming has become. Throughout Western Europe, for example, the survey found that viewers overwhelmingly choose to watch domestically produced programming in their own language. Table 6.1 (see pages 72–77) shows, by country and channel, both the five top prime-time shows by source and, of total broadcast hours, the percentage of domestic and imported programming.

The study makes one fact overwhelmingly clear: the near-universal preference for domestic programming at peak viewing hours. The exception seems to be in televising theatrical movies, through which Hollywood's popularity still can garner audiences worldwide, and the continued willingness of broadcasters to use cheap imports to fill out their schedules in non-prime-time hours. As the study itself concludes,

> despite the continued expansion of the international television market, opportunities for program sales to overseas markets were far from limitless. Indeed, the anticipated flood of U.S. programming on to foreign stations had failed to materialize and a growing number of indigenous producers were finding ready local buyers for their output.[30]

Table 6.1
Prime-Time Programming

Country	Channel	Hours/ Week	Domestic Programs (%)	Imported Programs (%)	Examples of Recent Top Shows in Prime Time (D=Domestic, I=Imported)	
Australia	Network 10	168	50	50	Hard Copy(composite USA/Aust.)	D/I
					E. Street	D
					Cops	I
	Sky Channel	100	90	10	Thoroughbred Racing	D
					Harness Racing	D
					Greyhound Racing	D
					World Title Boxing	I
					Australian Sporting	D
Belgium	BRT	90	62	38	Voetbal	I
					F.C. De Kampioenen	D
					Nieuws	D
	RTBF	86	60	40	Marche a l'Ombre	I
					Double 7 (game)	D
					Plein Cadre (magazine)	D
					Out of Africa	I
					Meurtre au Soleil	I
Chile	Channel 13	110	48	52	Sabados	D
					Teletrece	D
					Flash	I

COUNTRY	CHANNEL	HOURS/ WEEK	DOMESTIC PROGRAMS (%)	IMPORTED PROGRAMS (%)	EXAMPLES OF RECENT TOP SHOWS IN PRIME TIME (D=DOMESTIC, I=IMPORTED)	
DENMARK	DR	70	60	40	Wopklaret	D
					Gongehovdingen	D
					To Fag Frem	D
FRANCE	TF1	168	50	50	Football	D
					Le Grand Bleu (film)	D/I
					Les Mouettes (made for TV)	D
	Antenne 2	168	70	30	Bete et Mechant	D
					Jack l'Eventreur	I
					Papa est parti, Maman aussi	D
	Canal Plus	148	50	50	Operation Corned Beef	D
					Charlie I	
					Un Ange de Trop	I
GERMANY	ARD	110	80	20	Die Rudi-Carrell Show	D
					Sport-Football	D
					Tagesschau (news)	D
	RTL-Plus	150	48	52	Traumhochzeit	D
					Notruf	D
					Columbo	I

TABLE 6.1 (CONTINUED)
PRIME-TIME PROGRAMMING

COUNTRY	CHANNEL	HOURS/ WEEK	DOMESTIC PROGRAMS (%)	IMPORTED PROGRAMS (%)	EXAMPLES OF RECENT TOP SHOWS IN PRIME TIME (D=DOMESTIC, I=IMPORTED)	
GERMANY (cont.)	ZDF	90	80	20	Wetten daB...?	D
					Diese Drombuschs	D
					Ein Fall Für Zwei	D
INDONESIA	RCTI-PT	110	30	70	Knight Rider	I
					Mac Gyver	I
					Gara Gara	D
ITALY	TMC	131	56.33	43.67	La Piu Bella Sei Tu	D
					Galagoal	D
					No Zapping	D
	RAI-I	126	76	24	In Fuga Per Tre (movie)	D
					Achille Lauro 1	D
					Who Framed Roger Rabbit?	I
	Canale 5	168	62	38	Karate Kid III	I
					Paperissima (comedy)	D
					Altrimenti Ci Arrabbiamo	D
JAPAN	Fuji TV	165	94	6	Demande en Mariage	D
					Tuesday Night Special	D
					Tokyo Love Story	D

COUNTRY	CHANNEL	HOURS/ WEEK	DOMESTIC PROGRAMS (%)	IMPORTED PROGRAMS (%)	EXAMPLES OF RECENT TOP SHOWS IN PRIME TIME (D=DOMESTIC, I=IMPORTED)	
JAPAN (cont.)	NHK	583.3[1]	94	6	Nobunaga (samurai)	D
					Let's Compare (science)	D
					Evening News	D
	TV Asahi	168	96.5	3.5	News D	D
					Saturday DrThearte	D
					Sasurai Keiji	D
NETHERLANDS	NOS	174[2]	65	35	Journaal	D
					Ook Dat Nog	D
					Medisch Centrum West	D
NEW ZEALAND	TV3	100	40	60	60 Minutes	D/I
					Dinosaurs	I
					Give Us a Clue	I
NORWAY	TVS/Nordic	84	20	80	Glamour	I
					Primetime Movie	I
					Tour of Duty	I
	TV Norge	50	40	60	Casino	D
					Reisesjekken	D
					Films	I

TABLE 6.1 (CONTINUED)
PRIME-TIME PROGRAMMING

COUNTRY	CHANNEL	HOURS/ WEEK	DOMESTIC PROGRAMS (%)	IMPORTED PROGRAMS (%)	EXAMPLES OF RECENT TOP SHOWS IN PRIME TIME (D=DOMESTIC, I=IMPORTED)	
PHILIPPINES	Channel 13	98	76	24	Television Jesters	D
					All-Star Wrestling	I
					Lifestyle of Rich & Famous	I
PORTUGAL	RTP	229[3]	39[4]	38[4]	Rainha da Sucata	I
					Telejornal	D
					Os Simpsons	I
SOUTH AFRICA	M-Net	110	15[5]	85[5]	Midnight Caller	I
					Fresh Prince/Bel Aire	I
					Dear John	I
	SABC	222	50	50	Who's the Boss	I
					Telly Fun Quiz	D
					Major Dad	I
SPAIN	TVE-1	133.3	58.68	41.32	Uno, Dos, Tres (game)	D
					Se Armo El Belen (movie)	D
					El Ultimo Tranvia (musical)	D
SWEDEN	TV4	65	55	45	Beverly Hills	I
					Jeopardy	D
					Bingo Lotto	D

COUNTRY	CHANNEL	HOURS/ WEEK	DOMESTIC PROGRAMS (%)	IMPORTED PROGRAMS (%)	EXAMPLES OF RECENT TOP SHOWS IN PRIME TIME (D=DOMESTIC, I=IMPORTED)	
SWEDEN (cont.)	TV1000	168	15[6]	85[6]	Ray Bradbury Theatre	I[7]
					Mom P.I.	I[7]
					Doctor Who	I[7]
UNITED KINGDOM	BBC	242[3]	90	10	Eastenders	D
					Casualty	D
					One Foot in the Grave	D
	ITV	168	85[8]	15[8]	Coronation Street	D
					You Have Been Framed	D
					The Darling Buds of May	D
UNITED STATES	ABC	168	100	0	Roseanne	D
					Home Improvement	D
					Full House	D

Notes:
[1] Total for NHK's two channels, of which 325 hours a week is broadcast on its DBS channels (origin: D=44%, I=56%).
[2] Total for the broadcaster's three channels. [3] Total for the broadcaster's two channels. [4] Excluding news, sports, and advertising.
[5] Percentage of programming budget. [6] Figures for movies; for children's programming: D=50%; I=50%.
[7] Two shows & repeats/week. [8] Average breakdown of ITV stations.

Source: Chris Dziadul, "Ready for Primetime," *Television Business International,* May 1993, pp. 52–62.

WHAT KIND OF NEWS AUDIENCES WANT

The linguistic constraints outlined here are not the only audience challenges facing the global broadcasters, especially in the case of television news. The additional problem is that audiences around the world have their own preferences about what constitutes foreign news. In all countries, domestic news inevitably takes priority; but in the selection of foreign news, audiences are deeply influenced by neighboring states and regional interests. The globe is not of uniform interest, and the more distant the story, in general the less the audience interest.

Obviously, there are exceptional stories that bear global significance—the Gulf War, the Tienanmen Square uprising, and the near-coup in Moscow—were all treated by CNN International as global stories, and were indeed carried in one form or another by broadcasters around the world. But the amount of attention—and local interpretation of their significance—in fact varied widely, and were by no means normal in terms of the coverage routinely given to nondomestic news.

In 1991, the London-based International Institute of Communications examined news coverage from eighty-seven television newscasts around the world. What the study strikingly revealed is the regional focus of the coverage: in Latin America, 92 percent of stories covered Latin America; in South Africa, 80 percent were about Southern Africa; in Eastern Europe, 80 percent covered Eastern Europe; in Japan, 78 percent were about Japan; in the Middle East, 85 percent were about the Middle East; in North America, 80 percent covered North America; in Western Europe, 63 percent covered Western Europe.[31] In short, the overwhelming interest of audiences globally is not about global news per se, but rather in a much more focused sense of region as the relevant domain of concern. For organizations such as CNN International and other global broadcasters, this further erodes the mass-audience potential for a standardized global news wheel, and stresses the importance of national—and regional—broadcasters in delivering news to audiences that meet a broad audience interest.

Stated perhaps a little more formally, what we seem to observe empirically is the following:

1. As television markets, formerly controlled by public monopolies, are transformed into competitive markets (including both private broadcasters and commercialized public broadcasters), the

total number of broadcast hours, programs, the price paid for programming, and advertising spending experiences a substantial one-time lift.

2. The market then appears to stabilize at a rough new equilibrium level in terms of the number of broadcasters, hours, and ad revenues. New national broadcasters appear slowly, and existing broadcasters may in some cases fail (such as France's Le Cinq). Having taken a one-time jump in revenue and expenditures, at this new equilibrium, the broadcasters look for cost savings and controls to accommodate much slower growth in ad revenues.

3. Competition intensifies, as cable and satellite broadcasters enter markets and attempt to capture market share from the terrestrial channels. Outside the affluent countries that constitute the majority of domestic television revenues worldwide already, however, viewer ability to pay for these services is extremely limited. And even in the affluent countries, in Europe and Japan, willingness to pay for cable and satellite options nowhere seems ready to approach existing U.S. levels of acceptance (with a few, isolated exceptions).

4. Faced with terrestrial, satellite, and cable competition, the main terrestrial broadcasters (both public and private) focus on improved volume and quality of national-language programming. Viewers show a decided preference for this, over imports (with the exception of certain, generally American, movies).

5. In such a market, global broadcasting finds itself at a distinct disadvantage, particularly when it fails to broadcast in an audience's native language. Moreover, for global news broadcasters, there is the impediment of audience disinterest in a uniform global news agenda. This does not mean a failure for satellite-based broadcasting per se, but rather that it will be used more generally by nationally or language-based broadcasters to target specific national or linguistic audiences. For those insistent on the idea of a single-language satellite broadcaster offering a uniform global news package, audience disinterest raises daunting questions about how to expand beyond a distinctly limited niche market.

7

Reconsidering National Markets — and the Role of Global Broadcasters

Alvin Toffler, the futurist and author of *The Third Wave*, was invited as a keynote speaker recently to a convention of international television executives. He'd been a guest before the same group more than a decade earlier, and his speech—foreseeing vast and revolutionary changes—had been greeted with profound skepticism. This time, having survived the whirlwind emergence of satellite, cable, deregulation, and the like—the executives seemed readier to listen.

Toffler was at his futuristic best. Old-fashioned, over-the-air, locally based or network broadcasting, he firmly proclaimed, was "doomed," destined to become "a faint, forgotten blip in the image archives of tomorrow." Instead, the future belonged to a high-tech world of electronic interactivity and vast programming options, a world in which the individual viewer would be the producer. In place of mass media, Toffler assured his listeners, the next century belonged to its opposite, something he colorfully christened "individeo."

Les Brown, one of television's sagest critics, was in the audience, and found himself growing more and more frustrated. "My own reaction," he recalled later, "to Toffler's address was that it was good theater but questionable fortune-telling. Futurists tend to be more at home with technology than human nature, and it struck me that Toffler doesn't understand the dynamics of broadcast television at all." Brown is part of an emerging group of thinkers about global media who see localism—embodied in the old fashioned, over-the-air broadcaster—as having a much longer future than anyone ever expected.

"Broadcast television," Brown now believes, "has an edge on everything else in the marketplace today—or tomorrow—because, when it is working right, it is a complete service, responsive to the needs of its audience and capable of reacting to events." To Brown, the great difficulty facing would-be global satellite services, or even most cable systems, is that most of them are in fact not news services, but entertainment-based, and

> as incapable of interrupting themselves for a news bulletin as a video cassette. Any American watching HBO or MTV on January 16, 1991 would not have known that the country had gone to war in the Persian Gulf. Nor would they have known last May of the rioting in LA. I doubt that many residents of that city, behind their locked doors during those tense three days, were diverting themselves with cable programs or home video movies. Everyone in LA needed to be plugged in to the outside and for the most part they plugged in through the local broadcast stations.[1]

Brown's comments are worth pondering for a moment, because although he excludes news specifically from his implicit criticism of the new wave of satellite and cable technology, his criticism actually includes them in a crucial way when we think about the model of global news systems such as CNN or BBC as the future of television.

First, in looking around the globe, it is self-evident that there is an explosion going on—in the number of television sets, viewers, hours watched, channel choices, and variety of sources. For news broadcasting in particular, the good news is that television viewers throughout the world *want* more news—but also want it delivered in their own language, by newspeople who look and sound like them, and with an emphasis on local and national coverage.

No one can deny that the traditional national networks in the United States and the rest of the world are being challenged. But it is also the case that, measured in audience shares, they are withstanding the challenge. In the United States, for example, despite all the attention given to CNN, it is still the case that it rarely draws an active viewership one tenth the size of that watching one of the network's regular evening news broadcasts.

Outside the United States, in those markets where new private channels have sprung up to challenge the traditional state broadcasters, what's striking is how many viewers continue to choose public broadcast news as their first choice over any of the new private broadcast alternatives. In Britain, the number one news program is on BBC 1, in France on TF1, in Germany on ARD 1, in Italy on RAI, in Spain on TVE 1—all the supposedly "withering" public broadcasters threatened by the private-sector upstarts.[2]

This preference for established and recognizable news sources appears to be universal, and faces the would-be global news organizations with a set of significant challenges themselves. CNN International's vice president Peter Vesey has moved away from what was once seen as the direct competitive challenge his satellite-based global service once posed to the old-fashioned terrestrial national news organizations. He now says that was always just a "misunderstanding" of the role CNN International and BBC/WST could play: "Nothing we are doing could supplant the role played by the BBC or ITN in the UK or the German and French national broadcasters in their territory," he now insists.

But if the global systems *aren't* somehow aiming to displace the hundreds of national, terrestrial news systems now in operation (and growing steadily), what then is their function?

Are they what industry journalist Rich Zahradnik calls them, "office intercoms for the global elites"? Or can they hope in some way to comprise a "mass media" on their own? Reuven Frank, former head of NBC News, takes a distinctly matter-of-fact attitude toward the production of news in the years ahead: "News is a commodity," he says, "it's information retrieval. It's not a matter of better or worse; you sell it at the market price. It's like wheat."[3]

If Frank is right, the globals may be facing a distinctly uphill fight at becoming a commanding new form in the world of television news. The English writer and critic George Steiner has observed, in a different context, but with implications for the prospects of a uniform global news product, that

> each and every human tongue is a distinct window onto the world. Looking through it, the native speaker enters an emotional and spiritual space, a framework of memory, a promontory on tomorrow, which no other window in the great house at Babel quite matches. Thus every language mirrors and generates a possible world, an alternative reality.[4]

The relativity of language and culture is acting as a powerful gatekeeper, impeding the penetration of English-language enterprises such as CNN International and BBC/WST. As Christine Ockrent, a senior correspondent for RTF, the French network, says of CNN and its global coverage to date, it is "a U.S. channel with a global vocation, but which sees the world through an American prism. . . . When CNN's footage is not homemade in the U.S., it is homemade in some other country. That's not being international."[5]

A recent survey by the market research firm Eurodience of top news programs in five major West European countries where CNN International is available to viewers found that the nationally based programs overwhelmingly dominated their local markets, in some cases with individual programs capturing a thirty share or more in their market. (One sees this impediment at work even when language itself is *not* at work, but culture is: in British cable homes that receive both CNN International and the British-produced Sky News, the latter consistently outstrips its American competitor, even though most neutral observers consider Sky News an inferior information source.)[6]

An obvious alternative to an English-language global service is, of course, to tailor such a service into the vernaculars of the countries that lie beneath the footprint of whatever satellite carries that service. One example might be to produce a "finished" news program, consisting of a series of stories about news events around the world, but then "customize"—by dubbing or subtitling the program—into the various languages of the countries served.

Such an experiment is, in fact, under way in Europe right now. In 1993, the European Community launched Euronews, a five-language news channel, carried by satellite, and available currently to several million European viewers. The fact that such a system exists demonstrates its *technological* feasibility, but the problems that Euronews is already plainly showing also underscore how economics and competitive interests themselves act as a gatekeeper between what is technologically feasible and what is viable as a business enterprise.

From the start, key members of the European Broadcast Union (EBU) declined to participate in the service: the BBC opted out because of its interest in World Service Television; the two big German public broadcasters, ARD and ZDF, likewise passed because they in turn were actively involved in creating a new, German-language news channel, Weschienenkanel. That leaves the two largest language groups in Europe without domestic contributors to the channel, although Euronews broadcasts in both languages.

The Euronews channel itself is peculiar to watch, with a string of news stories running without an anchor person, and simultaneous narration provided off-camera. Operating on a $63 million EBU grant (with scant advertising), viewer acceptance seems extremely weak, at best, according to insiders. After its first year, the channel had overshot its budget by $10 million.

Geoff O'Connell, news director at the pan-European service Superchannel, is one among many skeptics who doubts whether Euronews is ultimately viable, given the EBU's own previous failure at Europa, its last attempt at pan-national programming—and Superchannel's own frustrations with a smaller-scale version of multilingual news. O'Connell freely admits that Superchannel's much more modest efforts didn't work, and pinpoints the reasons: a multilingual format "meant the product suffered, there were no on-screen presenters, one had to be reasonably neutral and you end up spending a lot of your cash just on translation." Peter Vesey laconically says much the same thing: asked whether Euronews would work, he said simply, "News is very expensive and you can go broke very quickly."

It is that issue—the *economics* of news—that again and again seems now to be shaping the evolution of the technologically feasible into the practically enduring. CNN itself can be credited with much of the current revolution not just in the technology, but the economics, of news gathering and broadcasting. Facing a comfortable, decades-old oligopoly of three dominant networks, Ted Turner transformed American television news not just by using a technologically new delivery system (where most of press attention and public commentary focuses), but in economically reshaping the cost of the news machine itself. Eschewing multimillion-dollar anchors and highly paid correspondents and their thickly staffed support organizations, he embodied the idea of "lean management," hiring at low wages and remaking work rules that had grown evermore complacent and expensive over nearly forty years of broadcasting.[7]

But, as in all newly competitive marketplaces, the innovator has had to watch as both older and newer competitors adopt and adapt a new leader's initial advantage. Just as over the 1980s, American manufacturing downsized staffing, installed computers, robotics, and just-in-time inventory practices, and turned to new work rules as a response to international competitors, so too American networks and overseas broadcasters—who might once have felt threatened by CNN and the perceived imminence of global competition—have turned to their own lean management style to guarantee survival (and profits) in an era of rapid change. And for these CNN competitors, the news from American manufacturing is good: last year, after more than a decade of battering, American autos began once again to gain market share against their once-seemingly invincible Japanese challengers.

What's happening globally, in the face of a potential challenge from global broadcasting, is a powerful reworking of the existing national, usually terrestrial over-the-air, systems. In real measure, the reworking had already begun in places like Europe *before* the advent of satellite broadcasting, as the domestic television markets were rearranged by the introduction of private channels and new demands for commercialization of existing public channels. It was here, in the introduction of competition through the redefinition of property to include the right of private use of public airwaves, that perhaps the real revolution lies.

But competition for acceptance by viewers requires a more complex idiom than technological feasibility suggests. Robert Ross, CNN's president, now acknowledges this: "CNNI in English is going to appeal to 2, 3, 4 percent of the market," he told an interviewer recently.[8] By itself, 2, 3, 4 percent of a global audience numbering several billion will leave Ted Turner a much richer man than he is today—if that is what CNN International ultimately achieves. In the meantime, however, not just Turner, but all would-be global broadcasters will have to adapt themselves to the reality of a world divided by language, income inequality, and government and private domestic broadcasters willing and ready to compete for their own audiences with the same technology and innovative capacities that have brought Turner and his CNN empire to where it is today.

Turner himself clearly recognizes this challenge, behind all the talk of global idealism and interest in the major questions of pollution, poverty, and war that still shape the daily lives of all too many of the earth's inhabitants. CNN International is already being customized in Spanish for Latin America; and in Germany, Turner has settled for a minority partnership in a German-language cable news channel instead of what he once promised would be a "Deutsch Network News (DNN)." Fitfully, he is building his international empire piece by piece, adapting as circumstance allows.

But this is not the one-world vision John Eger offered his listeners of "no barriers, no boundaries . . . [no] artificial divisions between the different people and places of the world." To the contrary, it is rooted in those very divisions, a recognition that, for the time being, global broadcasting will follow a pattern of multinational corporate expansion and alliance, bringing with it the age-old questions about culture and property and ownership that have marked the capitalist world since its birth.

In such a world, as this expansion takes place, the kind of technological fervor—what one pundit wryly christened "technoholism"—too often linked to the future of television will, as always, need to be tempered and reformed by the cooler claims of economic constraints. No doubt a hundred years from now, more people will be watching more channels that include more sports, entertainment, and news than ever before—including international shows and information seldom seen before by many viewers. But just as likely, those same people will still live in nations, with borders, and governments, and nationally rooted broadcast systems that provide most of what they see.

With news especially, the desire to know what is going on nearby, what is happening to our neighbors, what our own leaders and economy are doing, will always outdraw the distant plane crash or rumble of war or parliamentary folly. And to be told those things by people who sound like us, who look like us, who act like us likewise will endure.

In that sense, it may ironically be that the very technology that gave rise to the great promise of global television—through a process of economic and cultural transmutation—will actually spawn an unprecedented growth in local broadcasting. Linked together by that very technology, local broadcasters will find new and innovative roles to play, unimagined in the global debate that assumed their demise. Stranger things have happened. It wasn't long ago that the giant mainframe computers of IBM and a handful of other multinational giants seemed ready to define the "Computer Age," only to be struck down by the lowly personal computer. If the "Global Television Age" seems destined to share its time in history with the computer, its companion's chastening experience offers a salutary lesson of the need for modest claims about what lies ahead.

NOTES

CHAPTER 1

1. Ken Auletta, "Raiding the Global Village," *New Yorker*, August 2, 1993, p. 25.

2. For a sample of commentary on television and the Gulf War, for example, see Thomas Allen, et al., *CNN: War in the Gulf* (Marietta, Ga.: Turner Publishing, Inc., 1991); Robert Weiner, *Live from Baghdad* (New York: Doubleday, 1992); or Douglas Kellner, *The Persian Gulf War and Television* (Boulder, Colo.: Westview Press, 1992). The most excoriating, and informative, is probably John MacArthur, *Second Front: Censorship and Propaganda in the Gulf War* (New York: Hill and Wang, 1992).

3. These anecdotes are from John Lippman, "Tuning In the Global Village," in "Tuning In the Global Village: A World Report Special Edition," *Los Angeles Times*, October 20, 1992, p. H2.

4. John Eger, "Prometheus Revisited," Inaugural address, Institute for Humanistic Studies, Tokyo Institute of Technology, October 7, 1991. Eger is former senior vice president, CBS Broadcast, and managing director, CBS Broadcast International, as well as former director, White House Office of Telecommunications Policy. For a more academically sober, but nonetheless highly optimistic, assessment of global television's potential, see the late MIT sociologist Ithiel de Sola Pool's *Technologies without Boundaries* (Cambridge, Mass.: Harvard University Press, 1990).

5. Silvio Berlusconi, quoted in John Lippman, "Powerful Signals: A Look at Four Global Media Moguls," in "Tuning In the Global Village: A World Report Special Edition," p. H10.

6. Peter Fiddick, "The Global Village," *Gannett Center Journal*, Winter, 1989, pp. 92 and 99–100. See also Anthony Smith, *The Age of Behemoths: The Globalization of Mass Media Firms* (New York: Twentieth Century Fund Press, 1992), for a careful and critical look at multinational corporatization of media.

7. Ibid.

8. *TV Guide*, December 15, 1990, p. 3.

9. American television, of course, has not been a perfect model of laissez-faire competition, by any means; on the role of the FCC (and the federal

government in general) in the economics of U.S. broadcasting, see Bruce
Owen and Steven Wildman, *Video Economics* (Cambridge, Mass.: Harvard
University Press, 1992), for a representative account.

CHAPTER 2

1. Chris Irwin, "Address to the New Delhi Press Club," March 5, 1992
(London, BBC/WST, mimeo). Irwin is head of BBC/WST.

2. *The Economist Vital World Statistics* (New York: Times Books, 1990),
pp. 234–35.

3. Even in the United States, patterns of dispersal heavily follow income
lines. See Anne Wells Branscomb, "Who Owns Information," in John Pavlik
and Everette Dennis, *Demystifying Media Technology* (Mountain View,
Cal.: Mayfield Publishing Co., 1993), chap. 6.

4. Even in the United States, income has been a crucial factor in rate of
dispersal for communications technology: see John Carey, "Looking Back
to the Future: How Communication Technologies Enter American Households," in Pavlik and Dennis, *Demystifying Media Technology*, pp. 33–39.

5. Eli Noam gives an excellent summary of this pattern. See Eli Noam,
Television in Europe (New York: Oxford University Press, 1991), especially chap. 1.

6. In 1991, television broadcast revenues were the following (in billions):
NHK, $3.9; GE, $3.2; Capital Cities/ABC, $3; RAI, $2.9; CBS, $3; BBC, $1.7.
Turner Broadcasting reported $1.14 billion, of which CNN International
was only $28 million. See "Top 25 Public Broadcasters" and "Top 25
Private Broadcasters," *TBI Yearbook '93* (London: 21st Century Publishing,
1993), pp. 346–47 for size comparisons.

7. Singapore, with the proposed sale of SBC, and Mexico, with the sell-off
of Imevision, appear set to become the first countries to break up their
broadcast monopolies. See "Sale of the Decade," *Television Business
International*, May 1993, pp. 24ff, on Mexico, and *TBI Yearbook '93*, p. 161,
on Singapore. Brazil, though operating a public system, historically has
been dominated by private television, particularly the giant Globo.

8. The erosion of U.S. network audiences actually began in the 1970s,
as new independent UHF stations began broadcasting, but the erosion
accelerated through the 1980s with cable. On Europe's public stations,
see Charles Brown, "Public Service Blues," *Television Business International*, May 1993, pp. 64–72.

9. Noam, *Television in Europe*, pp. 8–9.

10. For an insightful look at the politics and economics of "technical" standard-
setting, see U.S. Department of Commerce, *Globalization of Mass Media*
(Washington, D.C.: Government Printing Office, 1993), especially pp. 37–42.

11. Bruce Owen and Steven Wildman, *Video Economics* (Cambridge, Mass: Harvard University Press, 1992) pp. 3–4.

12. And because sales effort is obviously not cost-free, the rational program producer will concentrate selling efforts in those markets first designed to yield the maximum revenue. The smallest markets will in fact either be ignored, or left to defray the program seller's costs by allowing buyers to initiate contact, either directly, or by transacting the sale at some public marketplace where seller's costs are distributed over multiple potential buyers. See National Academy of Television Arts and Sciences, International Council, *1993/1994 Almanac* (New York, 1994), for an extensive listing of the global television trade fairs each year.

13. See "Ways of Paying for Television in Europe," *TBI Yearbook '93*, pp. 353–56, for an overview and country-by-country analysis of license and advertising for public broadcasters.

CHAPTER 3

1. Bruce Owen and Steven Wildman, *Video Economics* (Cambridge, Mass.: Harvard University Press, 1992) p. 19.

2. Anton Lensen, *Concentration in the Media Industry: The European Community and Mass Media Regulation* (Washington, D.C.: Annenberg Washington Program, 1992), pp. 8–9.

3. Milton Mueller, "The Revolution in Telecommunications Property Relations," *Gannett Center Journal*, Winter 1989, p. 59.

4. "Exploring the World of Satellite Television," in "Tuning In the Global Village: A World Edition Special Report," *Los Angeles Times*, October 20, 1992, p. H12.

5. See R. Negrine and S. Papathanassopoulos, *The Internationalisation of Television* (New York: Pinter Publishers, 1990), chap. 3, for a discussion of the spectrum issue.

6. See Eli Noam, *Television in Europe* (New York: Oxford University Press, 1991), chap. 29.

CHAPTER 4

1. A more expansive definition of global television is offered by R. Negrine and S. Papathanassopoulos, although the terminology is slightly different—they use "internationalization" to describe what I call "global." See R. Negrine and S. Papathanassopoulos, *The Internationalisation of Television* (New York: Pinter Publishers, 1990), especially pp. 1–2.

2. Five countries—the United States, France, Italy, Britain, and Germany—account for 80 percent of all films that all countries import for

television broadcast. See UNESCO, *World Communication Report* (Paris: UNESCO, 1989), pp. 160–61. The percentage is for nonsocialist countries, prior to collapse of the Warsaw Pact.

3. Of course, given the extremely low sale price of programming to countries outside the industrialized core, low dollar volume in such trade understates the potential audience reached in these countries.

4. Off-the-record interview with author, May 5, 1993.

5. See Jean-Luc Renaud, "'Fortress Europe' Won't Be What Many Believed," *Television/Radio Age International*, April 1989, pp. 71–77, for an excellent summary of the shifting European market for U.S.—and European—programming.

6. This discovery of a preference for domestic programming is widely documented, and discussed later in this paper.

7. See Anton Lensen, *Concentration in the Media Industry: The European Community and Mass Media Regulation* (Washington, D.C.: Annenberg Washington Program, 1992), pp. 5, 8, 10.

8. Barrie Heads, "Co-productions: A Guide to Who's Doing What," *Television Business International*, October 1989, pp. 126–34.

9. See the EC study, "Television Without Frontiers" (Brussels, 1991), as well as a critical review of EC policy, cited in Lensen, *Concentration in the Media Industry*.

10. Neil Weinstock, *U.S. and International Programming* (Frost & Sullivan, New York, 1991).

11. Booz Allen & Hamilton, "Strategic Partnerships As A Way Forward In European Broadcasting" (London, 1991), available as a company-published report.

12. On European programming, see Lensen, *Concentration in the Media Industry*; on global programming, Neil Weinstock, *U.S. and International Programming*. Inevitably some small portion of this domestic programming does enter international trade, but the order of magnitude stands.

13. Jean-Luc Renaud and Chris Dziadul, "The TBI Primetime Programming Survey," *TBI Yearbook '93* (London: 21st Century Publishing, 1993), p. 306. For supporting data, see pp. 307–10.

CHAPTER 5

1. For a concise history of CNN, and a sense of Turner, see Hank Whittemore, *CNN: The Inside Story* (Boston: Little, Brown, 1990).

2. See "*60 Minutes* Exports Its Winning Formula," *Television Business International*, July/August 1992, p. 41. According to CBS, *60 Minutes* can be seen in thirty-five countries.

3. Lewis Friedland, *Covering the World: International Television News Services* (New York: Twentieth Century Fund Press, 1993), p. 53, note 29.

4. Ken Auletta, *Three Blind Mice: How the TV Networks Lost Their Way* (New York: Random House, 1991), p. 401.

5. $250,000 cited by Paul Amos, executive vice president of Fox Network, in Teresa L. White, "As Networks Stay Home, Two Agencies Roam the World," *New York Times*, March 8, 1992, p. 5.

6. Visnews lost money in 1987 and 1988, earned $5.9 million in 1990, then $2.5 million in 1991 (see ibid).

7. Ibid.

8. Whittemore, *CNN*, p. 33.

9. Friedland, *Covering the World*, p. 15.

CHAPTER 6

1. William Henry III, "Shaking Up the Networks," *Time*, August 9, 1982, pp. 50–57. See also Lewis Friedland, *Covering the World: International Television News Services* (New York: Twentieth Century Fund Press, 1993) p. 22.

2. Friedland, ibid., p. 36.

3. Johnson and Ross, in Friedland, ibid., p. 36.

4. Author interview with Peter Vesey, CNNI vice president, February 25, 1994.

5. Anita Sharpe, "CNN Sticks With Hard News as Ratings Fall," *Wall Street Journal*, June 9, 1994, p. B1.

6. Author interview with Peter Vesey, February 25, 1994.

7. Zahradnik, in phone interview with author, April 15, 1993.

8. On CNN hotels, author's phone interview with Peter Vesey, February 25, 1994; on BBC hotels, author interview with Hugh Williams, BBC/WST director of programming, April 13, 1993. Vesey claims to be optimistic about hotel fees, citing extensive piracy of CNNI's signal, which he hopes can be turned into paying hotel customers.

9. *TBI Yearbook '93* (London: 21st Century Publishing, 1993), p. 332.

10. Jean-Luc Renaud, "Still Room for Growth On Cabled Continent," *Television Business International*, December/January 1993, pp. 44–45.

11. MBC data from William Kennedy, chief operating officer, MBC, interview with author, May 4, 1993; Zahradnik, from interview with author, May 5, 1993.

12. Barbara Crossette, "Dish-wallahs Bring Satellite TV to India," *New York Times*, April 7, 1992, p. A3.

13. Nicholas Kristof, "Satellites Bring Information Revolution to China," *New York Times*, April 11, 1993, p. A1.

14. Jennie Kantyka, "CNN, BBC gear up for battle over Asia TV watchers," *Reuters Singapore*, October 3, 1991.

15. Author interview with Peter Vesey, February 25, 1994.

16. Jean-Luc Renaud, "Asian Satellites to Launch New Decade of Growth," *Television Business International*, April 1993, p. 50.

17. See "Datafile: Channel Guide," *Cable and Satellite Europe*, February 1993, p. 74, for a comprehensive list of European satellite channels and encryption status.

18. Marcus Brauchli, "A Satellite TV System Is Quickly Moving Asia Into the Global Village," *Wall Street Journal*, May 11, 1993, p. A1.

19. Chris Irwin, "Address to the Delhi Press Club," March 5, 1992.

20. See *TBI Yearbook '93*, on Starsat.

21. Author interview with Hugh Williams, May 4, 1993.

22. Julian Mounter, quoted in "If You Wish Upon a Star," *Television Business International*, May 1993, pp. 44–50.

23. "Murdoch's Asian Bet," *Economist*, July 31, 1993, p. 13.

24. Author interview, off the record, with senior Coca-Cola executive, April 19, 1993.

25. Author interview with Les Brown, August 4, 1993.

26. Author interview with Peter Vesey, February 25, 1994.

27. Rowena Evans and Jean-Luc Renaud, "The Last Frontiers of European Television," *Television Business International*, October 1989, pp. 68–76.

28. Lintas, Europe's largest media buyer, commissioned this study.

29. For 1989 study, see Jean-Luc Renaud, "Europe's Domestic Reality," *Television Business International*, December/January 1989–90, p. 43; for EBU study, see Anton Lensen, *Concentration in the Media Industry: The European Community and Mass Media Regulation* (Washington, D.C.: Annenberg Washington Program, 1992).

30. See Chris Dziadul, "Ready for Primetime," *Television Business International*, May 1993, pp. 52–62.

31. "The Global News Agenda," *InterMedia*, January–February and March–April, 1992.

CHAPTER 7

1. Les Brown, "Why Broadcast Television Keeps an Edge," *Television Business International*, July/August 1992, p. 11.

2. See Charles Brown, "Grinding News Into Profits," *Television Business International*, July/August 1992, p. 30.

3. See Lewis Friedland, *Covering the World: International Television News Services* (New York: Twentieth Century Fund Press, 1993), p. 39.

4. In Robert Stevenson, et al., *Foreign News and the New World Information Order* (Ames, Iowa: Iowa State University Press, 1984), p. 99.

5. William Henry III, "Man of the Year: History as It Happens," *Time*, January 6, 1992, p. 25.

6. Audience research by Continental Research, quoted in Charles Brown, "Grinding News Into Profits," p. 30.

7. See Hank Whittemore, *CNN: The Inside Story* (Boston: Little, Brown, 1990), especially chaps. 2–5 on how Turner restructured the costs of his network.

8. Friedland, *Covering the World*, p. 37.

INDEX

ABOUT THE AUTHOR

R ichard Parker is a senior fellow and lecturer at Harvard University's Kennedy School of Government, where he teaches on economics and the media. He has also taught at Oxford, Stanford, Berkeley, and universities in France, Spain, and the former Soviet Union. An economist by training, he is a graduate of Dartmouth College (B.A.) and Oxford University (Ph.D.). A former fellow at the Center for the Study of Democratic Institutions, he has held Marshall, Rockefeller, Danforth, Goldsmith, and Bank of America fellowships. He also has had a long journalistic career, first as associate editor at the *Center Magazine*, then as managing editor at *Ramparts*, and then as cofounder, editor, and publisher of *Mother Jones*, for which he also wrote a regular column on politics and economics for ten years. His books include *The Myth of the Middle Class* (Harper & Row) and *John Kenneth Galbraith: The Making of American Economics* (Viking, forthcoming).